LOST HERITAGE

LOST HERITAGE

The Heroic Story of Radical Christianity

Dr Kim Tan

Anchor Recordings Ltd

First published in 1996 by Highland Books, Two High Pines, Knoll Road, Godalming, Surrey, GU7 2EP.
This edition 2013 published by Anchor Recordings Ltd, 72 The Street, Kennington, Ashford, Kent TN24 9HS

Cover Design by Sally Maltby

British Library Cataloguing-in-Publication Data. A catalogue record for this book is available from the British Library.

ISBN: 978-1-909886-15-5

Printed by Createspace.

Table Of Contents

"What has been will be again; what has been will be done again; there is nothing new under the sun. Is there anything of which one can say: 'Look! This is something new'? It was here already, long ago; It was here before our time. There is no remembrance of men of old, and even those who are yet to come will not be remembered by those who follow."

Ecclesiastes 1:9-11

ACKNOWLEDGEMENTS

Someone else should have written this book. About twelve years ago, I suggested to my dear friend Dr Alan Kreider, a historian from the Mennonite tradition, that he write a book for the ordinary person in the Church. I felt then that we needed a book for non-specialists to help them trace their roots and appreciate the lessons to be learnt from church history. Having waited this long, I have taken up the task with more than a little apprehension. A scientist writing about church history sounds decidedly unwise. I have sometimes been critical of the "popularisers" of science. May the historians among the readers show some leniency towards this "populariser" of church history!

I would like to acknowledge a number of people who have had a significant influence on my life and helped to shape my thinking. It was Roger Forster who first got me excited about church history when he introduced me to Broadbent's *Pilgrim Church*. I am grateful to him for writing the Foreword. His devotion and energy continue to challenge me. Alan Kreider introduced me to the scholars' writing about Anabaptism. Meeting him and the Mennonite Church in London was my first encounter with Anabaptists in the flesh. I am grateful for his encouragement, guidance and inspiration over the years. I came to Guildford for university studies in order to sit under David Pawson's ministry. This was my alternative to attending Bible college. I have been greatly enriched by his teachings and continue to aspire to the high standards he has set in communicating God's Word. I am grateful for his constructive comments on the earlier draft of this work. I finally need to mention Thomas Chung, who has inspired in me a greater love for Jesus; his friendship over the years has been special. These men have fathered me in the faith - what a debt I owe them!

I am grateful to all those with whom I shared a community at Denzil Road, Guildford, for a number of years. Many of the views expressed here were formed in the environment of community life. Many have assisted with this project; for reading the manuscript, for helpful discussions and constructive criticism – many thanks. My special thanks must go to Andrea Klopper for reading the first draft and to Dr Richard Dixon for his editorial contributions. The responsibility for views expressed in this book, however, remains mine alone.

Most of the writing has been done at home often into the early hours of the morning. My long-suffering supporters have been my wife, Sally, and my sons, Ben and James, from whom have been heard the regular refrain: "Not Radical Church History again!" Thank you.

FOREWORD
by Roger Forster

There are at least three reasons why Kim Tan's book on Church History is necessary and important.

First "History teaches us nothing" is a well-known adage and at first sight might appear to contradict any claims for any value at all for such a book as this. However, mature reflection, of course, reveals the power of the assertion which any Christian, and certainly any philosopher since Socrates ought to acknowledge. To know that we know nothing, and history teaches us this, which is itself something, is the healthiest place to be if we wish to learn. Socrates took this place - so the story goes - and humility and teachableness are essential characteristics for any disciple of Jesus.

Much of what has been learned concerning the story of the Church, as indeed what is taught, has nothing to do with the people who sincerely seek to follow Jesus in discipleship. It is these disciples only which many people understand as the only true entity which should carry the title "Church", if Christ's definition of his people is taken seriously. Kim helps us to separate this wheat from the chaff, by clear and helpful parameters as to what truly might be called "Church" in Church History. He also identifies that it is popular ecclesiastical history which needs to be defrocked and shown for what it is. However, this requires a radically open mind in both writer and readers to finally decide what is the movement of God's people in the history of the human race, and what is its counterfeit which the enemy is certain to produce in order to keep men and women in darkness. No doubt not one of us will get it all right in trying to identify the true stream, but that is no reason for not starting and every reason for the humility enjoined in our proverb. As I welcome this book, I firmly believe there is need for many, many more of these radical interpretations of the history of the Church, so that we might better progress in the truth.

Secondly, "History is the story of great men". This assertion has also been repeated many times since it was first coined. Kim will demonstrate in this exciting saga that it is only a true statement if we understand greatness as taught and exemplified by Jesus. It is not the dictators, the warmongers, the rich and the political manipulators who determine finally the course of the human race, but those who are sent out as sheep amongst wolves and die daily, who are great because they are as little children and are great in Kingdom terms. The story of these little children or this "little flock", as Jesus calls it, is not only the true Church History but it is the story of the true vehicle through which the Spirit of God is guiding the human race and bringing it to its goal. The spilt blood of the martyrs of the Church is more effective than the spillers of their blood in getting God's will done.

Kim's interpretation of Church History will give good ground on which to refute the assertion of the nineteenth century theologian Willhausen "God works more powerfully in the history of the nations than in Church History". This popular and conventional view of power and its steering of history can be seen to be inadequate, if not completely erroneous in the light of the true Church History as Kim seeks to guide us through the vicissitudes of the Church's story. The truths for which the martyrs died are affecting the whole Church to a greater degree than ever, and are bringing history to its goal of Christ's return.

Finally, " Those who will not learn from history are condemned to repeat its mistakes". This perhaps is the most perceptive of the three assertion or reasons I have identified in commending Kim Tan's excellent book. He reminds us that Church History is like a commentary on the Bible. It is a commentary which shows the positive as well as the negative consequences of obedience or otherwise. One of the rare if not unique features of Kim's work is that after the presentation of Church history he draws out challenges, lessons, warnings and directions for us today.

This removes the somewhat misleading image of history, often born and matured while at school, where it is a boring subject without any application. Indeed we are back to the assertion that history teaches us nothing again, as our value judgement of its imposition upon us as children. However, if we would first know and then take seriously the terrible mistakes, misinterpretations and flagrant disobediences of the so-called Church of history, the more readily we will run into the place of the radicals - those who go to the roots of our faith in Scripture and the use of the Bible as their touchstone for truth- and act radically to avoid the failures of the past and be ready to obey the truer ways for the future. This would then hasten the day of the Lord:

"...What sort of people ought you to be in holy conduct and godliness, looking for and hastening the coming of the day of God, on account of which the heavens will be destroyed by burning, and the elements will melt with intense heat! But according to his promise we are looking for a new heavens and a new earth, in which righteousness dwells." (2 Peter 3:11-13 NASB).

And so we could write the final chapter of World and Church History in our time and in our lives! This book will help us in this highest of all endeavours.

Roger T Forster

July 1995

INTRODUCTION

It has been said that, next to the Bible, we can learn most about our faith through church history. It is the living commentary on the Bible, describing how men and women throughout the centuries have sought to work out their faith in various ways and cultures, under different political systems. It is the exciting story about the heroic efforts of countless thousands in their attempts to be true to the Scriptures; to practise a pristine, primitive, biblical and radical discipleship - often at great cost to themselves. Sadly, it is also the story of human failure. Again and again, we shall see the betrayal of biblical principles by segments of the church as they became increasingly wealthy and worldly, as they courted and flirted with the establishment of the day and ended up being assimilated into the status quo. It is a story of ferocious intolerance, greed and bloodshed - of politics and power side by side with the gospel of love and reconciliation.

The study of church history will elicit in us a mixture of reactions. On the one hand it will make us angry and sad. However, it will also excite us with admiration for the heroes and heroines of faith. Church history will challenge us about our own faith. Above all, it will cause us to stand amazed at the faithfulness of God in accomplishing His purposes on earth in spite of human disobedience and indifference.

As we look at church history in its different periods, we will constantly be challenged to ask the question "Did Jesus ever intend the Church to be like this?" Was it his intention that the Church should have elaborate buildings and a professional clergy?

Was his kingdom earthly and was Christendom therefore the right expression for the medieval Church? Christianity has been called a "bloody religion" because of the atrocities committed in the name of Christ. Was this the kind of church that Jesus wanted to build - one that sanctioned its adherents to murder "in His Name"? In each era, we shall describe the various deviations from the original blueprint laid down for the Church by Jesus.

One of the distinctive patterns of church history is the repeated emergence of protest movements in the face of increasing moral and spiritual decline within the established church of the day. In every generation there has always been an authentic witness of the gospel. Again and again, we shall discover that when corruption and moral laxity set in, when church structures become institutionalised, when a divergent model from that of the New Testament appears, there are always protests - from both inside and outside the institutional churches.

In an age of intolerance, when unity meant uniformity and conformity, such groups of dissenters were vilified and in many cases brutally persecuted and murdered. Branded as "heretics" and traitors, many thousands were subjected to torture, drowning and were burnt at the stake. There were instances of mass murders, genocides committed by Christians against other Christians. For centuries these dissenters were persecuted and hounded all over Europe, finding the occasional prince who offered them brief sanctuary. Much of the information about these dissenters comes from their enemies who, for obvious reasons, painted a rather black picture of them. It has been said that history is the propaganda of the victor: whoever wins writes history from their point of view. Much of the writings of the dissenters were confiscated and burnt so that their testimony could be distorted and misrepresented by their persecutors. In recent years however, through an examination of writings that had escaped destruction, scholars have shown that some of these "heretics" had lived a biblical faith and were more true to the New Testament than their persecutors in the established churches. They had maintained "a distinctive and indispensable testimony to essential aspects of Christian truth which, but for their faithfulness, might have been lost" (FF Bruce). We shall understand our debt to them when we realise just how many of the truths that are being recovered today were practised and preserved by these groups.

Known by different names in various countries, sometimes inside and at other times existing outside the state-churches, these groups share a common cause - a desire to return to the practice of some New Testament truth. Gottfried Arnold and Ludwig Keller in their pioneering works have proposed the thesis that the 16th Century Anabaptist movements had their roots in a true apostolic succession with the evangelical movements going back to the very earliest time of Christianity. However, even when no historical continuity between these groups can be demonstrated, there has nevertheless always existed a spiritual continuity, so that the true church never completely disappeared after apostolic times. They believed that the true church always existed somewhere, albeit driven underground and in hiding and therefore not always identifiable.

Several characteristics were repeatedly found among these groups - the separation of church and state, the church as a voluntary gathering of believers, mission, simple patterns of worship, Body ministry, emphasis on the authority of the Scriptures, the work of the Holy Spirit, the imitation of Christ, the mark of suffering. These were some of the hallmarks of the dissenters. Other traits were more specific to individual groups. For example, in feudal Europe the brilliant Czech reformer of the Unitas Fratrum, Peter Chelcicky, called for a dissolution of class distinction. Similarly Conrad Grebel, one of the Anabaptist leaders, campaigned for the abolition of interest rates and church taxes in order to relieve the burden on the peasants. There were some who also advocated pacifism and community of goods.

For convenience, I will refer to these groups as "protest", "dissenters" or "radical" groups ("radical" meaning "of the roots"). In addition to their protests against worldliness and moral laxity in the state-churches, we find them, on the positive side, recovering essential biblical truths and emphasising a discipleship based on the New Testament. Other names reserved for them include the Old Evangelicals, Radical Protestants, Non- conformists, the Brotherhood and the Believers' Churches. Many of them simply preferred to call themselves Brethren or Christians.

In the laboratory where I used to work, there is a copy of "MacArthur's Map of the World". This is a map with a difference - it is upside-down. It looks at the world as Australians "down under" see it. In a similar way, this book provides an upside-down view of church history, seeking to tell the story of the "losers" of history, the radical churches. But were they really "losers"? As we survey the spectrum of the Church today, from Roman Catholic to the charismatic independent nonconformist house churches!, we see that many of the truths preserved and practised by these radical groups are being restored. The persecutors - both Catholic and Protestants - are adopting the faith of those they once persecuted. From the point of view of "history", they may have been "losers". But from the perspective of eternity, they will be among those who will wear the victor's crown. We owe an enormous debt to their faithfulness in preserving the truth so that we may receive it in our day.

In the telling of the story, our focus will be on the radical churches. The story of the official Catholic and state-churches has been well documented and will be told only as it bears on our story. Obviously the abuses and failures of both the Catholic and Protestant churches have been included in the story. It would be difficult not to do so. However, it is not the author's intention to "victimise" any particular groups. This is history from an Asian perspective without the bias of Catholic/Protestant traditions. I trust that the accounts of the failures and abuses of the past will be balanced and fair. In a book of this nature, there will be many generalisations. One can always find exceptions to the rule, or exceptions which prove the rule! I have tried to be balanced with the generalisations made here. Whether I have succeeded is left to the readers to judge. The time period covered in this book ends with the early 1900s. The story of the Church in the twentieth century is vast and would require separate treatment. Of necessity, we shall be looking at church history in Europe because this was where most of the known radical groups existed.

This book is in two parts. Its emphasis will be to tell the story of the radical churches in order that lessons may be learnt for today. It is therefore more analytical than historical in its treatment. The first part of the book is historical, telling the story of the Church. The second part provides an analysis of the historical evidence and seeks to draw at lessons for today. For a detailed history of the Church, readers will have to turn elsewhere (see Bibliography). Readers who find the historical section "hard going" may like to skip to the second part of the book first. The lessons from church history are illustrated from the historical accounts. The analytical section may then inspire the reader to wade through the historical part of the book. I remember the excitement I felt when I first discovered these radical groups some 20 years ago. I realised then that I had discovered my spiritual roots. It was a homecoming and it was wonderful to feel at home with these heroes of faith who have gone before. May these pages inspire all of us to walk the path of the cross with our Lord.

1

THE NEW TESTAMENT CHURCH

The resurrection must have been the most incredible and bewildering event ever experienced by the disciples. After the ascension, they met together daily in one place for prayer and fellowship. During this period they must have retold the story of Jesus countless times, but the uppermost thought in their minds was probably the instruction by the Lord to stay in Jerusalem until they had received power from on high. Clearly they had no understanding of all that "being empowered" meant, but they waited. Then it happened. In the same way that God had breathed life into Adam (Gen 2:7) and Jesus had breathed on the disciples (John 20:22), so Jesus breathed the Holy Spirit from heaven on that early band of disciples (Acts 2:1ff). The difference from previous occasions was that this time it was a very dramatic act accompanied by the noise of a violent, rushing wind and flames.

This was the day of Pentecost. In post-exilic Judaism, Pentecost was celebrated as the anniversary of the giving of the Torah (Law) by Moses and confirmation of God's covenant with the new nation of Israel at Sinai. According to rabbinic teaching, Pentecost was also the anniversary of the covenant with Noah. It was therefore appropriate that God chose the day of Pentecost to give of his Spirit and to confirm the New Covenant of the Spirit (Ez. 36:25ff; 11:19; Jer. 31:31) to a new people-group or nation called out, from slavery to a kingdom of darkness, into his marvelous light. What kind of church was it at its earliest beginnings? To answer this question, we shall turn to the New Testament and seek to understand the nature of the Church and its practices in its early days. We shall call the Church of the first century the New Testament Church and examine it under its five essential features:

1. Evangelical

The New Testament Church was "evangelical" in doctrine. The first sermon by Peter began with an explanation of the apparent drunken state of the disciples by quoting from the prophet Joel and the Psalms. The sermon ended with these clear words:

"Therefore let all the house of Israel know for certain that God has made Him both Lord and Messiah - this Jesus whom you crucified."

Peter declared that God's seal of approval was evidently on Jesus through his "miracles, and wonders and signs which God performed through him in your midst" (Acts 2:22) as well as through raising him from the dead (Acts 2:24). Therefore Jesus is now both Lord and Saviour. In other words, he cannot be our Saviour if we do not acknowledge him as Lord. This was no gospel of cheap grace. On the contrary, it was a full-blooded gospel proclaimed with utter certainty by an eyewitness to the bloody events of the crucifixion.

In response to the sermon, all who heard were moved to ask the question: "What shall we do?" Peter's reply was that they should do two things - "repent and be baptised for the forgiveness of your sins" as a result of which "you shall receive the gift of the Holy Spirit" (Acts 2:38). He exhorted them "with many other words" to be saved from their sins. Three thousand responded and the Church was born. God, having ignited a spark in the band of eleven men, had now started a flame which would spread far and wide. The Church thus started out as a voluntary gathering of believers who had repented, been baptised and received the gift of the Spirit. This was the basis of entry into the believing community of God's people.

The New Testament Church was also evangelistic in practice. If these things about Jesus are true, they could hardly keep this discovery to themselves. So, from its birth, the Church began to spread its new-found faith with great enthusiasm, ingenuity and boldness.

> "And the word of the Lord kept on spreading; and the number of the disciples continued to increase greatly in Jerusalem, and a great many of the priests were becoming obedient to the faith." (Acts 6:7)

One of the great hallmarks of the early Church was its commitment to evangelism and mission. It understood this as a responsibility from the Lord to be his witnesses "both in Jerusalem and in all Judea and Samaria, and even to the remotest part of the earth" (Acts 1:8). This commitment was seen as the responsibility of every disciple, not just for a select few, resulting in the dynamism of its evangelistic efforts. The Church as described in the New Testament had a high view of the authority of the Hebrew Scripture. In his first sermon, Peter quoted from the Old Testament Scriptures and applied them to Jesus. Like Jesus, the disciples accepted the authority of Scriptures and gave themselves to the study of the Word. Furthermore Jesus had taught them to take a Christ-centred approach to understanding Scriptures (Luke 24:27). Jesus had fulfilled the Law and the requirements of the Old Covenant by his death on the cross. The Old Testament had now to be approached from this perspective. There was an eagerness among the believers for the Scriptures - both corporate ("They gave themselves to the apostles' teaching;" Acts 2:42) and in private study. It was said of the Berean believers that "they received the message with great eagerness and examined the [Old Testament] Scriptures every day to see if what Paul said was true" (Acts 17:11). Public teaching together with private study was the norm in the New Testament Church.

It is clear that the preaching and the studying was accompanied by instructions to obey and "to observe all that Jesus had commanded them" (Matt. 28:20). A "hearing-without-obeying" approach to the Scriptures would have been foreign to these Christians. Theirs was an obedience of faith. There was no conflict between faith and good works. True faith should result in good works: "Faith without works is dead" (James 2:17). A "silent faith", a faith that is not lived out, is no faith at all.

However, there was in the New Testament a conflict between faith and the works or acts of the Law. Can one be saved by observing the Law and carrying out the works of the Law? Is salvation only attainable for those who fervently keep every detail of the ceremonial laws? Jesus' answer to the lawyer (Luke 10:25ff) and Paul's lengthy argument in his letter to the Galatians both give an emphatic "no". A mere observation of the Law, or some ceremony or sacrament without faith, does not and cannot save us.

Regarding the relationship between Scripture and the oral Jewish traditions, it was clear that Jesus placed Scriptures above traditions. In a passage where Jesus denounces religious leaders of his day, he says:

"Woe to you, scribes and Pharisees, hypocrites! For you tithe the mint and dill and cummin, and have neglected the weightier provisions of the law: justice and mercy and faithfulness; but these are the things you should have done without neglecting the others." (Matt. 23:23)

Jesus spoke out forcefully against observing man-made traditions while neglecting the heart of Torah. The disciples learnt from his example. In the disputes between the Judaisers and Paul over the practice of circumcision and observance of days (Gal. 5:1ff; Col. 2:16ff), the disciples stood firm, appealing to the authority of the Scriptures. Traditions can be a help as well as a hindrance. There are good traditions which should be held on to, but when traditions take precedence over Scriptures, the erosion of our faith has begun.

2. Sacramental

The New Testament Church shared with the Jews the belief that God had given certain signs of his grace. While they argued that circumcision was no longer binding on Christians, the Church nevertheless retained two practices with Jewish roots - the washing of baptism, which had been part of the ceremony for accepting proselytes into the synagogue, and the bread and wine of the Jewish Passover.

Jesus was himself baptised in the Jordan by John the Baptist, as were probably all his disciples. During his ministry, his disciples baptised those who believed in him and this was continued into the book of Acts, where converts were baptised upon repentance of their sins and believing in the name of Jesus. It would appear that Jesus did not himself baptise anyone (John 4:2). There is evidence in Acts of a rudimentary liturgy for the very earliest period. All believers were asked the question "What hinders so-and-so from being baptised ?" (Acts 8:36; 10:47; 11:17; Matt. 3:14). In the case of the Ethiopian eunuch, Philip answered: "If you believe with all your heart you may." The Ethiopian then made a short confession and said: "I believe that Jesus Christ is the Son of God." (Acts 8:37) The New Testament Church did not regard baptism as merely an external sign of one's commitment of faith. Baptism was more than that. It was an identification with the death, burial and resurrection of Jesus and a means of receiving grace to live a new life. Whether it was essential for salvation was not a question that was raised in the apostolic age. The normal practice was that all who repented and believed on the Lord Jesus were baptised and incorporated into the Body of Christ.

One of the most descriptive comments about the life of the early Church is found in Acts 2:42: "And they were continually devoting themselves to the apostles teaching and to fellowship, to the breaking of bread and the prayers." Worship was a fundamental aspect of the life of the early disciples. Central to their worship was the breaking of bread. In fact, their worship was centred around the breaking of bread, where they remembered through their prayers and hymns the crucifixion and resurrection of Jesus. This was a simple meal carried out in private houses as was the setting of the Passover. The liturgy used would have been similar to that quoted by Paul in 1Cor. 11:24ff. In talking about the cup,

Paul writes: "This cup is the new covenant in My blood . . . , " echoing the words of Jesus (Matt. 26:26ff) when he referred to the cup as the "blood of the covenant, which is to be shed on behalf of many for the forgiveness of sins . . . " The apostle Paul saw the Lord's Supper as a covenant meal that can only be participated in by those who have committed themselves to the New Covenant community, the Church. In practice, only those who had been baptised were permitted to participate in the Lord's Supper. Like baptism, the breaking of bread was much more than an external ceremony or "memorial". The Lord's Supper was a means through which the efficacy and power of the death and resurrection of Jesus could be received by the believer. It was a way in which something of the life of Christ might be imparted to believers as they fed upon him. So strongly did Paul understand this communion with Christ he gave a warning that he who ate and drank in "an unworthy manner shall be guilty of the body and the blood of the Lord . . . and drinks judgement to himself"(1Cor. 11:76ff).

The New Testament Christians practised two sacraments. Both were rooted in Jewish history and were simple in form and practice. The Church was not anti-liturgical; some rudimentary liturgy was already developed for baptism and the Lord's Supper in the biblical accounts. Our Lord would certainly have celebrated the Last Supper as a Passover meal using the liturgy of the Passover. Neither were mere external acts. They were given as means of receiving God's grace. The recipients in some way received life as they participated in the sacraments by faith. The Latin word "sacramentum" originally meant an oath of allegiance (taken by a Roman soldier to his Emperor); but in the Church it is used of those actions which mediate the grace of God. The New Testament Christians were sacramentalists in the truest sense of the word.

3. Pentecostal

Without doubt, the Early Church demonstrated a "pentecostal" dimension in a way and to an extent that has not been seen since.

This was a community that experienced a supernatural dimension to their faith. They were walking as Jesus walked, teaching as Jesus taught, performing signs as Jesus had performed them and healing as Jesus healed. They were continuing the ministry of Jesus as his body on earth. Every ministry, gift and grace that was found in the Lord Jesus was now to be found in the Church. There was true Body ministry because the Spirit had been poured out on all kinds of nationalities and had given gifts to all members of the Body.

Many signs and wonders were taking place through the apostles and "everyone kept feeling a sense of awe" (Acts 2:43). Two of these are worthy of mention here. When God healed the man who had been lame from his mother's womb and who was known by everyone because he regularly begged by the Temple Gate, it was a spectacular miracle of healing in the same "league" as that of Jesus. No wonder all who knew the lame man were "filled with wonder and amazement at what had happened to him" (Acts 3:10). Peter seized the opportunity and preached about the crucified and risen Lord Jesus, the result of which was another 5,000 believers. On another occasion, Peter was given a word of knowledge about Ananias and Sapphira who had lied about their monetary giving. The judgment of God came upon them and they died while listening to Peter's rebuke. This is the only biblical account of being "slain in the Spirit"! The impact was immediate and "great fear came upon the whole Church" (Acts 5:5,11). The result was that "multitudes of men and women were constantly added to their number" (Acts 5:14). We should note that, on both occasions, the signs resulted in large numbers of converts. The purpose of these signs is to point to Jesus, the result of which is that many would be led to believe in Him.

What was the secret behind the power of the New Testament Church? The apostle Peter attributed this to being "baptised in the Spirit". But this baptism of Jesus, which was a corporate experience on the day of Pentecost, manifested itself in a number of ways in the Church. First, it resulted in a strong sense of the presence of God among the believers. Ananias did not lie to men but to God, because God was now dwelling among men. All subsequent moves of the Spirit in history would be characterised by this awesome presence and holiness of God. The Church was now the temple of God. So long as the presence of God was dwelling among them, the Church witnessed his power. However when the glory departed, and God moved on because he was grieved by its sins and disobedience, the power of God was lost too. The power of God, then as now, was inextricably linked to his presence. It was not an automatic right granted to the Church but something it had to preserve and conserve. Where the presence of God is, there is also conviction of sin. The closer we are to God, the more conscious we will be of our sins. He is the Holy Spirit. The emphasis then was as much on holiness as on spiritual gifts and power. This was a balance which was essential for the growth of the Church. Movements of the Spirit since then have been characterised by deep conviction and repentance.

Second, the coming of the Spirit resulted in a life of intense and persistent prayer by the disciples. Both extempore as well as set prayers were used. Acts 2:42 mentions the prayers, referring to the temple liturgy. The New Testament believers were clearly not afraid to use liturgy in their worship. They took the ancient liturgical prayers and revitalised them with the Spirit. Whatever the forms of prayer, they prayed them with power and intensity so much so that some of their prayer times were literally earth-shattering (Acts 4:31)! They did not have prayer meetings; rather when they met, they prayed. It was entirely natural and spontaneous for them to call on their Risen Lord for help and guidance.

Third, the baptism of the Spirit led the disciples to imitate the lifestyle of the Master. They lived a life freed from the materialism of the world. They had no wealth to speak of and therefore no human influence of any consequence. As a result, they were able to depend on God for his power. Peter said as much when he said to the lame man: "I do not possess silver and gold, but what I do have I give to you: In the name of Jesus Christ the Nazarene

- walk." (Acts 3:6). There seems to be an undertone in the New Testament linking the power of God with the simplicity of the believers' lifestyle. The coming of the Spirit affected the disciples in every area of life. It was not limited to their "spiritual" and devotional life. Their attitudes towards material things were also changed. Part of the secret of the Church's power must be because the disciples emptied themselves of worldly things in order that they might be filled with God's Spirit and power.

The pentecostal power also created something excitingly new in the New Testament Church. It created a new oneness which was literally out of this world! They were in one place, of one heart and mind, praying with one voice. Barriers were torn down between Jews and Gentiles, rich and poor, male and female. The rich, educated and influential did not dominate the Church. In fact the young Church was led by uneducated fishermen from the despised north. Servanthood and brotherhood were hallmarks of this first Spirit-filled community.

Last, a word about how the New Testament Church used the gifts of the Spirit. The disciples were aware that the gifts or tools of the Spirit were available to them for the task of building the Church. The gifts of the Spirit were, however, to be used in the context of evangelism and were not to be confined to worship meetings. Signs and wonders were given either to create attention for the preaching of the gospel or as a confirmation of the preached word. Glossolalia (speaking in tongues) was not the dominant feature of the Spirit's manifestations. The emphasis was on exorcisms, healings and prophecies. The kingdom of God had to come with demonstration of power by the Spirit. It can never be built with human abilities or military force. To this end, the New Testament Church has given us an example of how to use the gifts to spearhead the invasion of the Kingdom of God into enemy territory.

4. Radical

No one reading the first few chapters of Acts, however casually, can fail to be impressed by the radical nature of the New Testament

Church. It was one of the factors that drew me to the gospel many years ago. Here was a new humanity, the "Third Race" living radically differently from its culture. A new race of mankind had appeared in the Acts of the Apostles.

The disciples were supremely radical in their love for one another. All the historical barriers were torn down - racial, sexual and socio-economic. There were neither Jews nor Barbarians, male nor female, slave nor free. But all were united as one in Christ. Such was the extent of their new found love that they called each other "brothers" as they developed a new sense of family.

They sold their possessions and gave the money to the poor believers in the Church "so that there was not a needy person among them" (Acts 4:32ff). This was a direct fulfilment of God's promise to Israel, for the time when they would be in the Promised Land, "that there would be no poor among you" (Deut. 15:4) - so long as they continued to obey His instructions concerning the sabbath year. God required that every seven years the nation of Israel should rest for a year, release all its slaves and cancel all debts. This was radical stuff! Hardly surprising therefore that the nation chose to ignore these instructions. With two exceptions, once in Neh. 5:1ff and the other in Jer. 34:8ff, the Old Testament is silent about the nation of Israel obeying these sabbath year instructions.

The sabbath year was not the only programme that God had planned for Israel. Every three years the people were required to distribute one-tenth of their possessions, and every fifty years, there would be a jubilee year (Lev. 25:11ff). During the jubilee, the nation was instructed to rest for a year, release all slaves, cancel all debts and return all properties bought during the intervening fifty years to their original owners. No political party could hope to win power campaigning on such an agenda! But this was God and in these socio-economic programmes, we see something of his heart for his people. Well, did Israel keep the jubilee? You guessed right. It did not. What we have in the Acts of the Apostles is all the more wonderful then as we see the New

Testament Church practising the Jubilee. This was fitting as Jesus had announced his ministry with words about the Jubilee:

"The Spirit of the Lord is upon me because he has anointed me to proclaim good news to the poor. He has sent me to proclaim release to the captives and recovery of sight to the blind, to set free those who are downtrodden, to proclaim the acceptable year of the Lord." (Luke 4:17ff)

These are words from Isaiah 61 and were used as Jesus' "manifesto" for his ministry. The acceptable or favourable year of the Lord is the jubilee. The jubilee became regarded as the kind of society that Messiah would usher in, bringing shalom, justice and liberty.

Jesus' understanding of the anointing of the Spirit was that it would result in three things - preaching of the gospel, healings and social holiness. These three dimensions were seen in His ministry as well as that of the New Testament Church community. At the heart of these words from Isaiah 61 is that, when the Spirit comes, there will be true freedom. People will be set free from their sins through the preaching of the gospel; they will be set free from their sickness and demonic possessions through the healing ministry; they will also be set free from their material possessions through the acceptance of the jubilee. Here in the New Testament Church were a people set free from their sins, their sicknesses and their addiction to material wealth. This was true freedom by Jesus the liberator.

Of course the Church had to reinterpret the jubilee. Most of the believers did not own land or properties. But the principles of justice, of a redistribution of wealth, of discovering each other as the family of God, economic-sharing, of setting free all forms of captives and of *shalom* - these were taken up and worked out within the milieu of first century Palestine. Several more observations need to be made about this jubilee community in the New Testament. First, for them jubilee was to take place every day, not once every fifty years! Second, community was voluntary and not coerced. The disciples sold their land and gave willingly. Having received grace they showed grace to the household of faith. Third, community in the New Testament was

31

not Communism. There were those like Barnabas who still had wealth. Ananias and Sapphira were free to keep their properties had they so wished. Believers owned houses where the Church met. We are not to imagine some sophisticated charitable trust being set up to hold these properties for the Church! No such tax loophole existed. The New Testament community was worked out with individuals owning their private properties as the Israelites did when they entered the Promised Land. Private ownership was not a barrier to economic sharing. The important thing for them was that social holiness was inseparable from personal holiness. They lived a counter-cultural lifestyle distinct from those around them. This kind of lifestyle was so radical that they were later to be called "colonies of heaven". No wonder the pagans were attracted to them.

5. Organisational

The spontaneous and dynamic growth of the New Testament Church owed much to every disciple understanding his responsibility to be a witness. There was no official ordination for ministry. All who were baptised in the Holy Spirit had received gifts that were used in mission. The ministry of the gospel was conducted by the laity because the class of clergy did not exist. The Church practised the principle of the priesthood of all believers. Ordinary disciples could preach, teach, prophesy, heal, baptise and lead in the breaking of bread. This was true "Body ministry".

The New Testament Church was composed of men and women who had met the Lord and by a voluntary decision had joined themselves to a new society, an illegal new society. They would be terribly persecuted because for them only Jesus was Lord, not Caesar. There was a separation of Church and State because Jesus had said:

"My kingdom is not of this world, otherwise my servants will rise up and fight" (John 18:36);

"Render unto Caesar that which is Caesar's; render unto God that which is God's" (Matt. 22:21).

This was radically new. The Church was a whole new entity never before seen on earth. Membership of the Church was voluntary, without coercion, and was not due to one's birth, tradition or race, unlike other faiths. Someone born in an Islamic country today is automatically a Muslim, but someone born in Britain is not automatically a Christian. Islam has a sacral view of society where state and shrine are seen as one. The Old Testament was also sacral in practice. Christianity has a composite view of society where Church and State are separated. This was a major issue where aberrations and deviations from the New Testament understanding caused serious distortions and countless suffering for centuries. We shall return to discuss this in further detail in Part II: Lessons from Church History. The New Testament Christians were living in a period in which they did not have political, military or economic power. It was a minority faith and they were regarded as heretics and deviants.

Another feature of the organisation of the New Testament Church was the practice of founding new churches wherever believers were to be found. These churches were independent of any organisation, taught from the beginning to depend on the Word and the Holy Spirit and to be responsible to Christ, as Head of the Church. There was no centralisation of ecclesiastical authority. Their leadership was lay and corporate in structure. There was no distinction between laity and clergy because there was no class of clergy. There was a plurality of leadership in each local church. Each church had several leaders called bishops and deacons as well as several teachers and prophets (Acts 13:1). The word bishop was used to describe local church elders. Throughout the New Testament times, it did not have the meaning of the "episcopal" regional bishop. Whilst independent, they were nevertheless loosely connected with other churches and received frequent visits from wandering itinerant teachers, prophets and apostles.

* * * * * * * * * * * *

I don't idealise the New Testament Church; it had its share of problems, judging by the frank accounts of divisions, unfaithfulness, immorality and injustice in the New Testament. Without these teething problems, we would not have had the New Testament epistles. Nevertheless, we see here the Church as Jesus had birthed it in its pristine, simple but powerful condition despite its imperfections and immaturity. We see here a balance between the evangelical, pentecostal, radical and sacramental elements of the church. Word and Spirit went hand-in-hand. The sacramental was not uncomfortable alongside the pentecostal. It was only when all these features were emphasised in the Church that growth resulted. When the Church ignored certain features or over-emphasised one to the detriment of the others, it ceased to grow, becoming introverted and ultimately fossilised.

We learn from the New Testament Church what an authentic out-pouring of the Spirit is like. Signs and wonders are given not to entertain but for the expansion of the Church. Conversions follow the signs. There will be a marked sense of the awe and holiness of God leading to conviction of sin and repentance. Prayer is intensified and lives changed. Racial, social and economic barriers are torn down. The miraculous was not the most spectacular characteristic of the New Testament Church, the new found agapé love demonstrated through economic sharing and caring was. These same criteria may be used to judge all subsequent moves of the Spirit.

What we see then is the emergence of an exciting new community that would become a living advertisement of God's grace. This community would be the means to bless the nations of the earth. This was what Jesus left behind.

"It is surely a fact of inexhaustible significance that what our Lord left behind Him was not a book, nor a creed, nor a system of thought, nor a rule of life, but a visible community." (Newbigin)

2

THE EARLY CHURCH

With the death of the apostles, the Church entered a new phase of uncertainty about its relationship with the world. Of its mission to the world, however, there was no uncertainty whatsoever; this was a time of growth. How would the Church cope with this period of rapid expansion? How should it organise itself and yet allow room for the inspiration of the Spirit? How would the world react to this emerging movement? What was the nature of the Church leading up to the Constantinian era? To answer these questions, we shall draw on the writings of the Early Church as a source of information about the life and witness of the early Christians. This period up until Constantine will be referred to as the Early Church. We should, however, remember that whilst the New Testament is authoritative, the Early Church writings are not. But because of their proximity in time to the New Testament era, they can illuminate our understanding of the Scriptures and the life of the Church. The Early Church, as the immediate successors to the New Testament Church, inherited an infant. What would it grow up to be?

We shall look at the Early Church under the five headings previously outlined. In the main it continued the traditions of the New Testament Church but modified some practices because of the changing circumstances. There was the pressure from growing persecution, posing new questions about faithfulness. The new converts brought with them new problems via imported thinking and pagan practices. Some in the Church felt a need for a new organisation to cope with its rapid expansion. But what model could it adopt? Was there a biblical model of organisation or would any structure be acceptable?

1. Evangelical

Many excerpts can be quoted showing the "evangelical" nature of the faith in the Early Church. The second-century Christians may not have left us much of an account of their subjective experiences. They have, however, given us a wealth of information about the objective content of their faith. We shall quote from Tertullian's "rule of faith" as a representative of the apostolic faith of this period:

> "The rule of faith which is believed: there is but one God, and he alone is the creator of the world, who by the sending forth of his Word in the beginning brought the universe into being out of nothing; and this Word, called his Son, was seen in various ways in the name of God by the patriarchs, was heard always in the prophets, and last of all was brought down into the virgin Mary by the Spirit and power of God the Father, was made flesh in her womb and was born from her as Jesus Christ; thereafter he proclaimed a new law and a new promise of the kingdom of heaven, worked miracles, was nailed to the cross, was resurrected on the third day, was taken up to heaven to sit at the Father's right hand and to send in his place the power of the Holy Spirit to guide believers, and will come again in glory to take the saints into the enjoyment of life eternal and the heavenly promises, and to condemn the impious to everlasting fire, both parties being raised from the dead and having their flesh restored".
> *(Tertullian, Prescription of Heretics 13)*

This is a brilliant summary of the apostolic faith as handed down by the New Testament Church. There is a clear faithfulness to the biblical facts of the gospel. As we read the writings of the Early Church fathers, we are impressed again and again by their knowledge of the Scriptures. They undoubtedly regarded the

Scriptures as the authority for their beliefs and practices. Irenaeus and Tertullian, in opposing heretical teaching, formulated their summaries of Christian teaching into the "canon of truth" or "rule of faith". For both, however, the "canon of truth" was really the content of the Scriptures itself.

We see the Church faithfully preaching the apostolic faith and teaching its members the Scriptures. This was the safeguard against emerging heresies. Tertullian further describes the meetings of the Early Church in this way:

> "We meet together in order to read the sacred texts, if the nature of the times compels us to warn about or recognise anything present. In any case, with the holy words we feed our faith, we arouse our hope, we confirm our confidence. We strengthen the instruction of the precepts no less by inculcation; in the same place there are also exhortations, rebukes and divine censures."

An interesting feature of the service is the public reading of Scriptures. It must be remembered that the main opportunity for most Christians to become familiar with the Scriptures was through hearing them read in church. Therefore, the regular, consecutive reading of the Bible occupied a principal place in the service. This practice is similar to the regular cycles of Scripture readings in the synagogue. Although the Lord's Supper was celebrated only on Sunday, it is clear that the reading of Scriptures, preaching and prayers took place daily, such was the importance of the Scriptures to the life of the early Christians. So long as the Church continued to teach the Scriptures and encouraged its members to study them, there was a safety mechanism to preserve the truth. But there would come a time when the Scriptures would lose their importance in the meetings and when private Bible study groups would be made illegal, not by unbelievers but by the established churches. As we shall see later, it is from these private groups, meeting around the Word, that wave upon wave of truths from God's Word would be restored to the Church.

2.) Sacramental

The second-century document called the *Didache* instructs that baptism "ought to be done in 'running water'; while dipping in 'other' water and if need be, in warm water, and even more, mere sprinkling of the head are permitted only in case of emergency". Early church baptism was voluntary and only for those able to make a confession of their sins. This was continued into the early third century as seen by the writings of Hippolytus *(Apostolic Tradition ca.215)* and Tertullian *(On Baptism ca.205)*. The person wanting baptism, called the catechumen had to spend three years as a "hearer of the Word" before baptism. This was deemed sufficient time to examine the person's true character. On the Thursday before the Sunday of the baptism (Passover and Pentecost were the preferred times) they were bathed, exorcised and instructed to spend Saturday night in prayer and fasting. They were stripped naked, then baptised by immersion whilst confessing "I renounce you Satan, and all your service and all your works". The Didache seems to teach a "tri-immersion" - the believer was immersed three times; once each in the name of the Father, Son and Holy Spirit. Following baptism, they were anointed with oil and had the laying on of hands to receive the Holy Spirit. The service was completed with the kiss of peace followed by sharing in the first communion meal. It is clear from the practice of the early Christians that baptism was taken seriously and was for believers who were able to renounce the works of Satan in their lives. The fact that infant baptism crept into the church and became the dominant practice for centuries is part of the unfolding of this story. It seems clear, however, that up until the end of the fifth century, adult believer's baptism was the normal practice of the church. Infant baptism up until then was a sideshow to the main baptisms, which were of catechised adults.

The Early Church, on the whole then, maintained the apostolic practice of believers' baptism by immersion. However, unlike the New Testament Church where those who repented and believed on the Lord Jesus were immediately baptised, it would appear that new converts had to spend several years in preparation before baptism. This change may be due to a number of factors. Primarily this practice arose because the Church needed to be convinced of the genuine nature of the "enquirers". We have to remember that Christianity was an illegal religion and the Church existed and grew as an underground movement. It had to be sure that those who wanted to join were sincere in their intentions and were not "spies" sent to infiltrate the Church. The persecuted Church in China and the former Soviet Union know how important this "screening" process is. Dr Alan Kreider has shown that the Early Church services were not very "seeker-friendly". New catechumens could only

> "participate in the first part of the Sunday worship of the Church. Week after week they enter the door, but only just. For, although . . . they will hear the reading of the Scriptures and the expositions of the presbyters, they will be reminded that they are only catechumens. They must leave before the mysterious rites that follow".
>
> (Laing Lecture, 1994).

The mysterious rites refers to the Eucharist, in which only those who had been baptised could participate. Deacons were placed at the door as "bouncers" to screen all those entering! All these demanding procedures were introduced into the persecuted Early Church to ensure that only those who were genuine became members. But perhaps there is another reason. The New Testament Church was largely Jewish in its membership. Gentile converts were likely to have been proselytes with some knowledge of the Old Testament Scriptures. The Early Church, however, was now more and more gentile in its composition. Coming from such pagan backgrounds, there was a need for a period of teaching as well as an examination of the person's life. Are there signs of repentance? The Apostolic Tradition asks:

> "Have they lived good lives when they were catechumens? Have they honoured the widows? Have they visited the sick? Have they done every kind of good work?"

Churches working among animistic tribal people today follow this same practice of delaying baptism. In Borneo, for example, the practice is to have a period of instruction and examination of the new convert's life before water baptism can take place. The converts are expected to live like Christians and show evidence of faith.

We turn now to the sacrament of the Lord's Supper. The common name used by second-century writers is Eucharist, from the Greek *eucharistia* meaning thanksgiving. The oldest celebrations of the breaking of bread as recorded in the Gospels and Acts of the Apostles took place in the setting of an actual meal in private homes. The Eucharist in the Didache was also set in the context of a social meal. Only in the second century did the fellowship meal develop separately into the "love feast" because of abuses such as those observed in Corinth (1Cor. 11:20ff). The Eucharist remained the climax of the worship service and was a fellowship meal for those in the baptised community alone. The bread and the wine were ordinary food. Justin Martyr used the common word for "bread" and states that the wine was the ordinary table drink, not straight wine but wine mixed with water. This was to defend Christians against charges of misconduct when they participate in this "mysterious rite".

Throughout this period, baptism was understood as a means of grace or sacrament; as an instrumental means of regeneration. Irenaeus taught baptismal regeneration as did Justin Martyr, who based his doctrine of baptismal regeneration on John 3:3,5 and Isaiah 1:16-20. Also from the earliest times the Church felt the celebration of the Supper was much more than a mere act enabling it to mentally remember the life and death of Jesus. This sacramental understanding was continued through the period of the Early Church.

The danger, however, with the sacramental aspect of the Church is that it can either degenerate into informality or grow into sophisticated institutionalism. Both were dangers experienced by the Church through its history. With the first, the sacred things of God are trivialised. With the other, the simple things of God are institutionalised and substituted with superstitions. The Early Church observed two sacraments - baptism and the Lord's Supper. This was later to be expanded to seven sacraments before the radical churches restored the Church to its New Testament understanding. The early sacraments were very simple in form but were later elaborated into sophisticated ceremonies with elements of superstition underpinned by doubtful theology. It came to be believed that the water used in baptism had "magical" powers of regeneration irrespective of faith, and that the bread and the wine were "magically" changed to the substance of the body and blood of Christ. This became known as the doctrine of transubstantiation. In the Early Church, the sacraments were administered by ordinary people, not by the professional clergy, because there were no lay/clerical distinctions. However, for a "magical" view of the sacraments to take root, a professional class of clergy had to be created. Soon it was only the clergy who could perform these "magical" acts.

Let us make some further observations about the worship services of the Early Church. The Roman officer, Pliny, after investigating the Christians made the following report to Emperor Trajan:

"...they [the Christians] were in the habit of meeting on a certain fixed day before it was light, when they sang in alternate verses a hymn to Christ, as to a god, and bound themselves by a solemn oath, not to any wicked deeds, but never to commit any fraud, theft or adultery, never to falsify their word, nor deny a trust when they should be called upon to deliver it up; after which it was their custom to separate, and then reassemble to partake of food - but food of an ordinary and innocent kind. Even this practice, however, they had abandoned after the publication of my edict, by which, according to your orders, I had forbidden political associations. I judged it so much the more necessary to extract the real truth, with the assistance of torture, from two female slaves, who were styled deaconesses; but I could discover nothing more than depraved and excessive superstition." *(Pliny, Letters)*

This was the testimony of a man who had used torture to extract the truth from Christians. Despite some scholarship issues relating to this text, it draws attention to a number of features of Early Church worship.

We see the Christians meeting on a "fixed" day (Sunday) at dawn. Most of them were slaves and had to work seven-day weeks (no Sabbatarians here!). They met before starting work. Secret societies in the Roman world required an oath from members to observe their statutes. Concerned that the Christians might pose a political threat to the Empire, Pliny was naturally interested in the content of the Christians' membership oath. What he described sounds like the instructions to a baptismal class of new converts. They bound themselves by a solemn oath to live righteously. The gathering later in the day (evening) was for dinner, the main meal. This was most likely the "love feast". Pliny was obviously impressed by their singing of hymns to Christ as their God.

Whilst truly free in the Spirit and charismatic in nature, the early Christians were not afraid of forms and traditions so long as they were genuinely handed down by the Lord or were inspired by the Spirit. They sang the Psalms in typical Jewish fashion. The inspiration of the Spirit also created many new hymns, some of which are recorded in the New Testament. The ancient Psalms and the "modern" hymns were used together. The earliest surviving Christian "hymn book" is the Odes of Solomon from the second century. This is a collection of 42 songs used by Syriac-speaking Christians. Let us quote the "Greek Evening Hymn" to give us a feel for the worship of this period. This has been universally acclaimed as one of the most beautiful pieces from antiquity:

"Gracious light of the holy glory of the immortal, heavenly Father, the holy one, the blessed one, Jesus Christ!

Having come to the setting of the sun, seeing the evening light, we hymn the Father and the Son and the Holy Spirit of God.

Worthy are you at all times to be praised with holy voices, Son of God, giver of life; therefore the world glorifies you."

It would appear that the early Christians were anything but anti-liturgical. There are many examples of "set" prayers. They recited the prayer that Jesus taught them. They confessed their faith through liturgy, an example of which was simply the Eucharistic prayer "Maranatha. Our Lord ‚come". Like the New Testament Christians, the worship of the Early Church was simple and very similar to the synagogue service. It included Scripture readings, interspersed with Psalm chants, preaching, praying and giving. The Lord's Supper had its own prayers, Scriptures and liturgy. Hymns and liturgy were vehicles to express praise to God and worship was open for all to participate. Later in the fourth century, however, the emphasis was placed on the music and the singing; church music became a genre of its own, monopolised by a professionally trained clergy with the congregation largely as spectators.

One final comment about the absence of musical instruments in the worship of the Early Church. The emphasis of the hymns was on the words. Melodies were adapted to the words which were chanted and were not bound to a rigid form of tempo.

"The priority of the words and the forms of rendition ensured that the singing was done without instrumental accompaniment. Indeed, an instrument had no function in these simple chants with their emphasis on the content of praise. There is no certain evidence of the use of instruments in the Christian liturgy until the later Middle Ages. Because of the associations of musical instruments with immorality in the pagan world, the Church Fathers took a dim view of them in any setting and allegorized the Old Testament references to instruments in worship." (Everett Ferguson).

3. Pentecostal

Contrary to popular thinking, the power and the gifts of the Spirit did not die out after the apostolic age. Irenaeus in the second century spoke of those who prophesied and had visions. He also referred to a continuing healing ministry and even the raising of the dead. Consider the following:

Irenaeus: "[those] who through the Spirit do speak all kinds of languages and bring to light for the general benefit the hidden things of men and declare the mysteries of God."

Justin Martyr: "It is possible now to see among us women and men who possess gifts of the Spirit of God."

Tertullian: "There is among us a sister whose lot it has been to have gifts of revelation, which she experiences by ecstasy in the Spirit during the regular services of the Lord's day in the church . . . Whether it is when the Scriptures are read, or the Psalms are chanted, or sermons are preached, or prayers are sent up, all such occasions are supplied with visions." (On the Soul 9:4)

The Didache informs us that all catechumens after their three years preparation were baptised. This was followed by anointing with oil, exorcism and the laying on of hands for the receiving of the Holy Spirit. This was still part of the process of becoming a disciple.

With time however, there was a decline in the use of spiritual gifts. This slide was linked to the increasing institutionalism of the Church. Inspirational giftings gave way to institutional qualifications in the leadership. Prophecies and healings continued to be emphasised but not tongues. By the late second century, evidences of God's power had become less frequent. By the third century, these had largely ceased, although healings continued, now especially associated with relics and pilgrimage places. But they continued to exist into the third and fourth centuries, often surviving on the margins of the Church's life in radical groups such as the Montanists (see below). This was a "charismatic" group which was supressed by the ever more institutional Church. The gifts of the Spirit probably persisted in mainstream church life for longer than scholars like to think. It is inconceivable that the Church could have grown during this period in such a dynamic way without the Christians knowing the power of the Spirit.

4. Radical

The Early Church continued the distinctive radical lifestyle of the New Testament. By its acts of mercy and sacrificial giving, it demonstrated a new kind of love that the pagan world had not witnessed before. An outstanding example comes from Carthage. During the outbreak of plague in AD 251, Christians cared for the sick and buried the dead when many inhabitants had fled. With corpses piling up in the city, Cyprian urged the Christian community to stay, bury the dead and care for the sick and needy. This was an opportunity for the Christians to stay and love their enemies who had recently been persecuting them. With such testimonies, the Church continued its growth.

Caring for the disadvantaged, acts of mercy and community of goods were part of the practice of the Early Christians as evidenced by the writings of the Early Church fathers:

> "And instead of the tithes which the law commanded, the Lord said to divide everything we have with the poor. And he said to love not only our neighbours but also our enemies, and to be givers and sharers not only with the good but also to be liberal givers towards those who take away our possessions."
> (Irenaeus, ca. 200, *Against Heresies* IV.xiv.3)

> "Widows are not to be neglected . . . Do not despise male or female slaves, but neither should they be puffed up . . . They (the slaves) are not to ask to be ransomed from the common treasury lest they be found slaves of their desires" (Ignatius, ca. 200, To *Polycarp* 4)

Justin Martyr has given us a wonderful picture of a normal early Christian service which includes the distribution of food:

> "On that day which is called after the sun, all . . . gather together for a communal celebration. Then the memoirs of the apostles or the writings of the prophets are read, as long as time permits. After the reader has finished, the one presiding gives an address, urgently admonishing his hearers to practice these beautiful teachings in their lives. Then all stand together and recite

prayers. After the end of the prayers, the bread and the wine-mixed-with-water are brought and the one presiding sends up prayers and thanksgivings to the best of his ability. The people chime in with an Amen . . . Then takes place the distribution, to all attending, of the things over which the thanksgiving has been spoken, and the deacons bring a portion to those absent. Those who prosper-and who so wish-contribute each one as much as he chooses to. What is collected is deposited with the one presiding, and he takes care of the orphans and widows, and those who are in want on account of sickness or any other cause; and those who are in bonds and the strangers who are sojourners among us. He, in short is the protector of all those in need. We hold this common gathering on the day called after the sun, since it is the first day on which God, transforming darkness and matter, made the universe and Jesus Christ our Saviour rose from the dead on the same day." (Justin, ca. 150, 1 *Apology* 67)

"These contributions (that is, put into the Church's treasury) are the trust funds of piety. They are not spent on banquets, drinking parties or dining clubs; but for feeding and burying the poor, for boys and girls destitute of property and parents; and further for old people confined to the house, and victims of shipwreck; and any who are in mines, who are exiled to an island, or who are in prison merely on account of God's Church - these become the wards of their confession. So great a work of love burns a brand upon us in regard to some. "See" they say "how they love one another" . . . So we who are united in mind and soul have no hesitation about sharing property. All things are common among us except our women. (Tertullian, ca. 200 *Apology* xxxix.5-11).

"Let the strong take care of the weak; let the weak respect the strong. Let the rich man minister to the poor man; let the poor man give thanks to God that he gave him one through whom his needs might be satisfied. (Clement of Rome, ca. 100, 38:2)

"All things are common, and the rich are not to be avaricious .

. . And it is not right for one to live in luxury, while many are in want. How much more glorious is it to do good to many than to live sumptuously! How much wiser to spend money on human beings than on jewels. (Clement of Alexandria, ca. 200, *Instruction* II.xiii.20.6)

Here were Christians set free from their possessions so that they would be able to share and give radically to support the poorer members, orphans, widows, prisoners and even non-Christians. During this period, the concept of "the offering", as opposed to tithing, was also developed. Those who came to church would bring money as well as food-oil, cheese, olives, bread, wine-as their offering. The poor brought water for diluting the communion wine. By the third century, clothes and shoes were also mentioned. These offerings would be placed on a table by the entrance and distributed by the deacons to the needy, including any absent from the meeting for various reasons.

How extensive the community of goods was practised is not clear. Tertullian and Clement of Alexandria were obviously among those who adopted the New Testament practice. What is clear, however, is that the sharing of material goods was universally taught and practised by the Early Church. In this, the Early Christian had faithfully maintained the spirit of the jubilee.

Not only were the Early Christians radical in the matter of their possessions. They were different in their whole way of life. The *Letter to Diognetus* from the second century gives us a vivid insight into the lives of the Early Christians. The unknown author is seeking to explain to Diognetus

"what is the secret of the affection they (the Christians) have for one another":

"Christians are not distinguished from the rest of mankind by either country, speech or customs; the fact is, they nowhere settle in cities of their own; they use no peculiar language; they cultivate no eccentric mode of life . . . Yet while they dwell in both Greek and non-Greek cities, as each one's lot was cast, and conform to the customs of the country in dress, food and mode of life in general, the whole tenor of their way of living stamps it as worthy of admiration and admittedly extraordinary. They reside in their respective countries, but as aliens. They take part in everything as citizens and put up with everything as foreigners. Every foreign land is their home, and every home a foreign land.

"They marry like all others and beget children; but they do not expose their offspring (that is, killing them). Their board they spread for all, but not their bed. They find themselves in the flesh, but do not live according to the flesh. They spend their days on earth, but hold citizenship in heaven. They obey the established laws, but in their private lives they rise above the laws. They love all men, but are persecuted by all. They are unknown, yet are condemned; they are put to death, but it is life that they receive . . . Doing good, they are penalised as evildoers. The Jews make war on them as foreigners; the Greeks persecute them; and those who hate them are at a loss to explain their hatred . . . " (Letter to Diognetus)

These were people who belonged to another kingdom and what was more, living as citizens of the heavenly kingdom. It is particularly striking that, unlike the pagans, the Christians did not kill or abort their infants. They shared their possessions but not their wives, as Tertullian also noted. Christians were marked by their marital fidelity. There was an emphasis on the imitation of Christ. To the early disciples, being Christ-like was everything. They followed Jesus in his suffering, non-violence and enemy-loving. The instructions given to the disciples at the Sermon on the Mount were an important foundation of their radical discipleship.

Let us finally observe the Early Christians' attitude to military service and violence. *The Apostolic Tradition* of Hippolytus contains a list of professions "proscribed" for Christians. Surprisingly the list include teaching because they were required to teach polytheism as a part of the curriculum. But others listed include being charioteer, a gladiator, a pagan priest, a magistrate and a military man. All converts undergoing catechism were asked about their profession. If the candidate was in one of these professions, he would be asked to cease his profession or be refused baptism. In the case of those in the army, they could be catechised only if they promised not to kill. Whilst most of the church leaders such as Origen and Hippolytus were consistently pacifist in their views, it is clear that Christians did indeed serve in the army. Tertullian admitted as much in his letter to Marcus Aurelius:

"We sail with you, fight with you in the army, we farm and trade with you . . . " *(Apology)*

and yet later maintained a clear anti- militarist position, arguing against a Christian serving in the army.

Initially the number of Christians in the army was small. But it grew steadily in the third century, and when Constantine recognised the Church in the fourth century the situation altered radically. By the fifth century, there was a total reversal of the anti-militarism of the Early Church. In 416, Theodosius decreed that only Christians could be in the army.

5. Organisational

The Early Church, as we have seen was largely faithful to the apostolic faith that it had received with respect to the evangelical, sacramental, pentecostal and radical aspects of church life. However, in the organisation of the Church, we detect significant changes during this period that would prove harmful for it.

The end of the first century saw the Church with a New Testament pattern of organisation. The Didache describes the transition from the itinerant, inspired ministry of the apostles, prophets and teachers to a local ministry of bishops and deacons. Provision is made for the travelling prophet or teacher to settle in the community and be supported by the Church. The local uninspired men now succeed to the ministry of these men in public teaching and conduct of worship:

"Elect therefore for yourselves bishops and deacons who are worthy of the Lord, men who are meek, not lovers of money, true and tested. For they minister to you the service of the prophets and teachers. Do not look down on them, for they are your honoured men along with the prophets and teachers," *(Didache)*

In some instances, the travelling evangelist or teacher himself becomes the local bishop of the church he had started:

"Consider. ..cities where Christians are not yet found, some one arrives and begins to teach, labours, instructs, leads to the faith and finally becomes himself the ruler and bishop for those whom he taught."
(Origen, *Homily on Numbers*)

The bishops were not merely there for the purpose of government of the local Church. They were regarded as those who "possess the succession from the apostles" (Ireanaus, *Against Heresies*), carrying out the ministries of the prophets and teachers. Clearly many of these local bishops had great prophetic and teaching ministries judging by the likes of Irenaeus, Tertullian, Origen and Cyprian.

Local churches were initially led by a plurality of bishops or elders who were assisted by deacons. This was, however, to change in the early part of the second century. Ignatius of Antioch, writing to the churches of Asia Minor, described a threefold ministry of one bishop, elders and deacons in the churches. Whereas "bishop" and "elder" had referred to the same function, now a differentiation was to take place with the bishop presiding over the local elders or presbyters. By the middle of the second century, this organisation was generally accepted in the western part of the Empire. The emergence of the single bishop of the local Church was the first step towards the creation of an institution.

As churches in the large cities grew, presbyters (elders) were assigned to particular assemblies in the city. The bishop in turn presided over the presbyters in the diocese. This was a significant shift in the organisation of the Church. It represented the basis for a structure of church government that would be increasingly centralised. Christians in the non-urban areas lacking their own bishop would look increasingly to the city church for leadership.

This rise of regional bishops was to develop further in the third century. The bishop of the capital city began to assume a leading position among the bishops of the provinces. These "metropolitan bishops" approved and ordained the new bishops for the provinces. The metropolitan bishops of the Early Church became the forerunner of the medieval archbishops in the western Church. The independence of the local church was being gradually eroded.

Other changes were also taking place during this period. The role of the bishop, whether regional or metropolitan, was becoming more official and less functional. The emphasis was more on government and less on ministry. The inspirational leadership of the New Testament started to give way to the institutional leadership of the Early Church. The Church was showing signs of developing into an institution. As all this was happening, a subtle change was also taking place with a growing distinction between clergy and laity. The officers of the Church began to be differentiated from the people (Gk. *laos* from which laity is derived) in the Church by status and function. By the time of Cyprian in the third century, the language of "priesthood" from the Old Testament began to be used as titles for officers of the Church. One can view this period either as the emergence of the priesthood in the Church or as the emergence of a laity without any ministry. Both groups were novel. They represent a serious deviation from the New Testament model. The priesthood of believers was abandoned during this period.

As the Church gradually became more institutionalised and less inspirational, changes also took place regarding the role of women. Recent historical research has demonstrated that in the first years of renewal movements, women are disproportionately involved. When the emphasis is upon Spirit-gifting and spontaneous ministry, women have been at the fore. But when the emphasis is placed upon structures and institutions, men take over and exclude the women. This was true of the first two centuries of Christianity. Women were involved as long as the Church emphasised the prophetic gift, but as it became institutionalised, they were progressively marginalised. The sociologist Max Weber put it this way: "as routinisation and regimentation of community relationships set in, a reaction takes place against pneumatic [spirit] manifestations among women". History is written by winners and until recently they have all been male! I believe we need to recognise the role of women in the Early Church. However, was this restricted only to the inspirational ministries or were they involved in church government? Setting aside whatever ounce of male chauvinism I might still have in me, one must still ask why it is that both in the New Testament and the Early Church writings, the role of bishop or elder is invariably in the masculine? Prophetesses (such as Perpetua, martyred in 203) and deaconesses (such as the two tortured by Pliny) are mentioned. Even female apostles are possible if one takes the text in Romans 16:7 to read Junia (feminine) which was more common, rather than Junias (masculine). John Chrysostom in the fourth century commented that Junia was both female and an apostle. More research is needed to clarify this issue of gender and leadership.

What was the Church like at the end of this period? It was strongly evangelical and evangelistic - growing in number. It retained elements of the radical and sacramental with certain modifications to meet the challenges of its day. By the late second century a pattern of formal catechism had been developed. While largely faithful to the New Testament vision, we also see that during the Early Church period, various shifts in understanding the nature of the Church were already present. Distortions on a number of issues can already be detected by this stage - distinction between clergy and laity, the emergence of priests and regional bishops. We see here the beginnings of the Church institution and with this development, a corresponding decline in the pentecostal power of the Church. The Church will be seen to become less and less dependent on God and more reliant on its organisation.

3

HOW THE CHURCH
CONQUERED THE WORLD

(AD 30 - AD 400)

We forget too easily that Jesus initially gave the task of taking the gospel to the world to eleven men. They were not well educated; they had no influential backers and no political base. They were nobodies, outcasts among their own people, coming from a peasant background, from an inferior part of the Roman Empire. The probabilities of success were stacked against them. How could they succeed in their mission to "conquer" the world? But they did.

The rise of Christianity during the first 300 years can only be described as meteoric. During this time it changed from a minority movement to take over the Roman Empire, not with an army but with the gospel. The Church fought valiantly and won. During this period too, we see a shift of focus from Jerusalem to Rome; from the capital of the spiritual world to the capital of the "secular" world.

The first century provided some invaluable aids to the spread of the gospel. Conditions were suited to the missionary endeavours of the Early Church in various ways:

1) *Pax Romana* : The spread of Christianity would have been more difficult had Jesus been born half a century earlier. The whole known world was under the rule of one power, Rome, and for the first time there was a peace unparalleled in history. No passports were required for travelling so the apostles could move about freely.

2) *Roman infrastructure* : During the expansion of the Roman Empire, thousands of miles of roads were built so that effective communications could take place. The early apostles took advantage of these infrastructures to spread the gospel.

3) Greek culture : As a result of the conquests of Alexander the Great, the Greek language had almost become the universal common language. This was still true even when the empire came under Roman rule. It was no coincidence that the New Testament was written in Greek for ease of dissemination.

4) Jewish diaspora : The Jewish synagogues scattered across the Empire were often the first places where the early Christians preached the gospel. The Jews of the diaspora were more open to the claims of the gospel than the Jews of Jerusalem. Furthermore, they had created an interest among the gentiles for the Jewish faith to the extent that there were many proselytes. Such Jews and proselytes were among the first converts of the gospel outside Jerusalem.

5) Moral weakness of the Empire : The spiritual and moral bankruptcy of the Roman Empire was an ideal platform for the preaching of the gospel. The abuses of the rich and powerful had created many disaffected people, including many poor people among whom the gospel was good news.

Even with these conditions, the rapid spread of the gospel was still a miracle. It was carried by ordinary men and women to different parts of the Empire. The Church at that stage was not composed of many influential people but of ordinary citizens and slaves, of whom there were some six million in the Empire. They had no buildings, no headquarters or central committee to dictate directives. Local groups of Christians with their own leaders were directly responsible to Christ and were obedient to the guidance of the Holy Spirit. There was a vitality and freshness about this embryonic movement; a simplicity and spontaneity that was at once attractive and powerful; an integrity of life that commanded the respect of all - including those who would put them to death; a *koinonia* or fellowship expressing their love and unity that was to invite the jealousy of the Emperor Julian: "These wretched Galileans; they not only feed their orphans and widows, they are feeding ours as well." The spread of the gospel can best be seen from the testimony of their enemies. For the first 20 years after the crucifixion, there are no documents with any mention of Christ and his disciples. This was an infant minority protest movement within Judaism which had not yet caused any ripples. During the next 50 years, we have the writings of the Christians themselves forming what is now the New Testament. This indicates that the movement had grown to the extent that believers now wanted to have copies of the "teachings of Jesus" as recorded by the apostles who had accompanied him. But still there was not a word from any outside writer. Then in the second century, we begin to get a stream of largely disparaging comments about the Christians from Roman writers such as Tacitus, Suetonius, Celsus, Lucian and Pliny the Younger. By this time the Christians were sufficiently large in number to cause the establishment of its day to take notice. All this in 100 years, starting with eleven men! The period AD 50 - 300 was not, however, without its problems. The young Church was seeking to maintain its new identity under pressure from many fronts. Jesus had warned his disciples that they would find themselves in a very hostile environment but that they were not to be alarmed because he would send them another Comforter, just like himself, who would be with them to the end of the age. He had also given them the commission to make disciples of all nations and assured them of his authority to such an extent that the gates of Hades would not overpower them. Its status as *religio illicita* brought upon the early converts the ten major persecutions of 64-300 during which time thousands were martyred, causing Tertullian to remark: "The blood of martyrs is the seed of the Church." Yet the Church has never grown as quickly as in the first 300 years of its history (until today!).

The church had to brace itself for battle on a number of fronts: religious, philosophical, moral, spiritual and physical. None of these proved unique to the Early Church but have been subsequently fought by the Church up to the present time.

1. Religious battles

One of the earliest dangers facing the Church was syncretism, a mixing of other religious thoughts with Christianity. The early followers of Jesus were Jews, as were the early converts of the Church. Among them, there was a temptation to retain the observance of the Jewish oral traditions in the Church. These "Judaisers" required all gentile believers to be circumcised and keep the Jewish laws. There were strong pressures for Christianity to remain a Jewish sect. Even after the destruction of the Temple in AD 70, the Essenes attempted to get Christians, who were Messianic Jews, to return to Judaism.

This crisis of identity was finally resolved at the Council at Jerusalem (Acts 15). The edict of the Council, Paul's epistles and confrontation of Peter (Gal. 2), and the Letter to Hebrews, all stated that Jesus was the fulfilment of the Law and that God had opened a new and better way into His presence through the Cross. Animal sacrifices, circumcisions and other Jewish practices were therefore no longer required. This expression of Judaism, centred around the Temple and legalistic observance of human traditions which had become attached to the Law, was obsolete and regarded as a corruption of the true faith handed down by the patriarchs and prophets. Christianity would not mix with this legalistic form of Judaism or any other religion. The new wine could not be contained in the old wineskin.

The Christians were later offered a niche in the Roman pantheon for an image of Jesus, along with the other gods. This would have legalised Christianity as a religion and could have prevented the terrible persecutions. Yet the Christians refused. Had that happened, world and Church history would have been quite different.

This is not to deny the inevitable Jewish flavour in the new Christian faith, rooted as it was in the Old Testament and the concept of a Jewish Messiah. Christianity is Jewish. We in the Church have been grafted into this Jewish faith. Our God is the God of Abraham, Isaac and Jacob. This has often been forgotten and has led to the tragic anti-Semitism of the Church throughout its history. But a day will come when the two faiths will converge as we usher in the Second Coming of the Messiah.

The book of Revelation tells us that at the end times there will be a movement towards a whole new world religion. This is a modern-day battle we have to fight.

2. Philosophical battles

In the main, these battles were against the Greek-influenced philosophies. The intellectuals and scholars were a major threat because they could out-argue the Christian. The Church responded to this battle with words and the pen, and raised up many able teachers and apologists. Some of these theologians and apologists are listed in the Appendix. The major philosophies that these early Christian apologists encountered included :

a) Gnosticism (1st Century)

Gnosticism was a dualist Greek philosophy that separated matter, considered evil, from spirit, which was regarded as good. The Gnostics believed that the way to get up each rung of the ladder to God was through acquiring secret knowledge. Docetism was a particular form of Gnosticism. It denied that Jesus, the *Logos* (which is good) could have been a real man (which is matter and therefore evil). Docetists believed that Jesus was a phantom and that where he walked he did not leave any footprints behind. The prologue in John's Gospel was written with them in mind. When

John said that the Word *(Logos)* became flesh *(sarx)* which is evil, Gnostics must have been affronted. The rest of the Johannine writing and Colossians also repudiate this philosophy.

b) Marcionism (2nd Century)

Marcion was a wealthy Christian ship owner from Asia Minor who moved to Rome in140. Marcion's problem was that he did not like the God of wrath in the Old Testament. He applied the scissors to the Bible to remove the books that he found offensive and found that he could not stop. Paul was Marcion's greatest hero and it was no surprise that he ended up with a Bible containing only the ten Pauline epistles (minus the Pastoral epistles and Hebrews), Luke and Acts and two Gods - the God of the Old Testament and the God of the New Testament. He was ex- communicated in 144. His rival church movement was widespread in many parts of the Empire and was numerous and influential for nearly two centuries.

Marcionism is not dead. It is very much alive in certain theological schools of thought. What Marcion did not appreciate was that when it comes to understanding the Bible you have to approach the Old Testament via the New, and the New Testament via the Old. The Old Testament has to be interpreted in the light of the New because it completes and fills out the Old. "The New is in the Old concealed; the Old is in the New revealed." The purpose or aim of Torah and the Old Testament is Jesus. They are incomplete until Jesus. The Old Testament is dynamic, not static; moving all the time in the development of its revelation towards the Messiah.

c) Manichaeism (3rd Century)

Mani was born into an aristocratic Parthian family in southern Babylonia in 216. He was converted at the age of 24 and went on a pilgrimage to India before returning to the Persian Empire where he had access to the royal household. His teaching was a mixture of Gnosticism, Zoroastrianism, Buddhism and Christianity and was highly mythological. He attributed the creation and matter to a dark and evil power, not to God. According to him, there was an eternal Light imprisoned in creation and "Jesus,the Brilliant Light" was an example of the suffering of imprisoned Light in matter. In practice, the followers of Mani ate no meat and abstained from sexual life as a process of liberating themselves from matter. Arrested by Karter, the Zoroastrian priest, and imprisoned in chains, Mani died in 276. However his teachings spread everywhere in the Roman Empire and were even found in China in the 8th century.

d) Arianism (4th Century)

Arius was a presbyter at Alexandria (died 336) and was a fellow student with Eusebius of Nicomedia under Lucian of Antioch. He denied the divinity of Christ and the Trinity and regarded the Logos as a created being intermediate between Creator and creation. Arianism was condemned at the Council of Nicea in 325 after the vigorous defence of the faith by Athanasius. However, Arius' teaching gained even more popularity after the death of Emperor Constantine in 337 because his son and successor Constantius supported Arius. Arius' friend, Eusebius of Nicomedia, was influential because of his contact with the imperial household and his post as patriarch of Constantinople. He had the honour of baptising Constantine just before his death and had great influence with Constantius. Modern equivalents with Arian-like Christology are found in the teachings of the Jehovah's Witnesses and Christian Science sects.

The Church fought this philosophical battle in four ways:

1) It decided to put together all the books that went back directly to the Apostles. By around 200 the canon of the New Testament was largely completed as the basis of faith. It was regarded as Scripture and was the sole authority in all matters relating to creed and conduct.

2) It stated the apostolic faith in Creed (Latin *credo* means I believe). The Nicene Creed which condemned Arianism was the first one to be formulated. "I believe in God the Father Almighty, Maker of heaven and earth .. .." It is interesting

to note where the Early Church placed its emphasis. In the Nicene Creed, there were seven words relating to the death and resurrection of Jesus - suffered, crucified, dead, buried, descended, rose again, ascended. There was not a single word about his life except his birth. For the Early Church, the Cross and the Resurrection were central to faith.

It is striking that the Nicene Creed, unlike the earlier "rule of faith", had nothing to say about the life and ministry of Jesus. The Nicene Creed was a "womb to tomb" statement of belief. Some scholars have suggested that it could be because the radical teachings, healings and miracles of Jesus were too radical for an established Church. This is an interesting view which merits consideration.

3) It called Councils at regular intervals, not to organise the Church but to consolidate the faith, discuss issues of interpretation, and defend the faith against heresies.

4) It established "bishops" with teaching authority as a means of combating heresy. Much of the writings of the Early Church were directed towards teaching the apostolic faith in order to refute emerging heresies.

What are the philosophical and intellectual battles of today? They include Existentialism, Relativism, Universalism and the New Age. The battles on this front are as fierce and as subtle as they were during the time of the Early Church. We need to think ourselves clear on these issues.

3. Moral battles

Greek philosophy with its dualist emphasis tended to separate creed from conduct. How you lived and what you did with your body was not related to what you believed. Moral laxity was everywhere and corruption was rife. It was an enormously unjust society with six million slaves living in misery and a privileged class living hedonistically.

The letters to the Corinthians show the battle that the Early

Church had in maintaining its Christian piety. Initially the problem was with the immorality of the unbelievers. There were cities such as Corinth and Ephesus, prosperous commercial centres with large temples to goddesses such as Aphrodite and Diana, where temple prostitution was practised. Gradually as the church became established, the immorality and worldliness within the Church became the subject of much conflict. From its earliest days, the Church had to contend with straightening out the lives of converts with such backgrounds. To a large extent, that was why most of the epistles were written. Not only did they correct wrong doctrines, they also corrected wrong conduct. They admonished those who neglected the poor, the widow and those imprisoned. They sought to encourage a just and sharing community through the collection of monies (2 Cor 8-9) because corruption and injustice were as immoral as sexual misconduct.

With time, the corruption and moral laxity moved from the world into the Church and finally affected its leaders. When challenged by radical groups about the immorality of the priests administering communion, the Catholic Church responded by saying that the character of the priest was unimportant because the sacraments themselves had the power to save the individual. Martin Luther himself, in emphasising faith to the exclusion of works, also fell into this way of justifying the Protestant priesthood.

The apostles and the apostolic fathers never saw a dichotomy between creed and conduct. The example of Jesus and the New Testament epistles clearly show that both are necessary and advocate a high moral standard of living. The Early Church fought this battle through Bible teaching and by example. We have a similar moral battle on our hands today. The Church needs to give a clear lead in this issue both by word and deed. Morality is slowly being eroded in our churches so that we do not speak out concerning the breakup of the family, abortion, fornication, adultery, neglect of the elderly, unemployment, conduct of government and business. But we must not speak out against these matters without being prepared to offer practical assistance.

The early Christians did not just speak out against the injustices of the Roman society; they provided practical care for the poor, the elderly and the disadvantaged.

4. Spiritual battles

Witchcraft, sorcery, necromancy, idolatry, temple prostitution and secret religions were rampant throughout the Roman Empire. In a sense, this was the easiest of the battles because the early Christians knew the power of the Holy Spirit in a way that has not been experienced until this century and only in certain parts of the world.

The Acts of the Apostles throbs with thrilling stories of the power of the Spirit overcoming the powers of darkness. The early Christians evangelised in the same way with the Word and works of miracles. However, as the Church became more and more worldly in its ways and structure, there was less and less evidence of the power of God at work. This is still the case today. The power of God is linked to our piety. The Early Church did not seem to have too many problems on this battle front. It exercised the authority provided by its Lord.

5. Physical battles

Hard though this may be, it was nevertheless the most straight-forward of all the battles fought by the Early Church. The philosophical and intellectual battles were harder, more subtle, often coming in the guise of Christianity. The Church never used force to convert in the first four centuries, even though violence was used against it. Why were the Christians so hated? Not just because of the malicious rumours about the Christians but because Jesus had said: "They have hated Me without a cause . . . ."(John 15:25). The assault on Satan's kingdom would be met by strong opposition as Jesus himself had found.

Once the Church became largely gentile, Christianity and Judaism began to diverge with the result that the Church lost its protection under the wing of Judaism. Christians also refused to offer incense on the altar to the "divine" Emperor, an act which was interpreted as unpatriotic. In this way, the official Roman attitude to Christianity became rapidly less favourable. Rejection of the Roman gods was felt to threaten the peace and prosperity that the gods bring, and refusal to worship the Emperor was an act of treason.

As has been said, between 64 to 300, there were ten periods of persecution in which many thousands died. The first great persecution occurred very early - at around the time of Paul's death under the Emperor Nero in 64. Nero was said to have fiddled during the great fire which swept through Rome. Fourteen out of 17 districts of Rome were burnt and rumours soon spread that Nero had started the fire himself:

> "To be rid of this rumour, Nero fastened the guilt on a class hated for their abominations, called Christians by the populace. Mockery of every sort was added to their deaths. Covered with the skins of beasts, they were torn by dogs and perished; or were nailed to crosses; or were doomed to the flames. Nero threw open his garden for the spectacle and exhibited a show in the circus." (Tacitus, ca. 100)

The Christians served as convenient scapegoats because they were of a minority faith that refused to participate fully in the activities of the society. They were regarded as outsiders, and the common people of Rome, eagerly repeating scandalous rumours about them, were hostile towards them. The Christians were easy targets for the imperial authorities.

This was followed by the persecution during the reign of Marcus Aurelius (161-80). He was responsible for setting up the cult of Sol Invictus; sun worship, which he brought back following his conquest of Syria. December 25 was his birthday and was also regarded as the birthday of the Sun. Two centuries later, the church would assume this date as the birthday of Jesus - a clear example of syncretism. Emperor Decius (249-51) also carried out a vicious and systematic persecution of Christians. The final major persecution took place during the time of Diocletian

(284-305). Many of his slaves and servants, as well as his wife and daughter, were believers. He ordered all churches to be burnt, Christians killed, those in high positions in government and army sacked and all clergy imprisoned. This was Satan's final fling of the period. He knew he was losing.

Comment on martyrdom

This was a tragic period in the history of the Church. Tens of thousands died savage deaths. Precisely how many we will never know until we meet them again. While many kept the faith and died as martyrs, others gave in. This created a problem for the Church at the end of the persecution: should those who had denied and compromised their faith be accepted back into the Church? Some churches said "yes", but others said "no". This issue tore the Church apart and still does today in countries where Christians have been persecuted such as Russia and China. This is a difficult matter for which much grace and wisdom is needed.

Despite the sufferings, this was also a glorious period. The more Satan sought to eliminate the Church by violence, the more it grew. The Church grew not only numerically during this time, but also in maturity. Throughout history, God has used suffering as a means of bringing the Church into maturity.

The Constantinian Change
Constantine is a bit of an enigma. One either sees him as a champion of Christianity, or the changes that happened due to his patronage as a perversion of Christianity. Was he a champion or a corrupter of the faith? In the past, most historians viewed Constantine in a positive way. However, scholars have begun to take a more critical view of this era as one of significant change that seriously altered the life and testimony of the Church.

Following his father's death, Constantine was proclaimed emperor by his father's troops at York in 306. In the struggle for supremacy of the Western empire, he emerged triumphant by defeating Maxentius in 312 at the Milvian Bridge on the edge of Rome. According to Eusebius and Lactantius, Constantine saw a vision of a cross in the noonday sky 'above the sun' and the words "In this sign conquer". Constantine put this sign on his standard, went into battle and won. As was the habit of all the superstitious emperors before him, Constantine felt that the sign of the cross had brought him victory and therefore adopted the Christian faith. Thus was installed the first "Christian" emperor of the Roman Empire. A new hybrid of "Christian sacralism", (see section on "Church-State relationships") of church and state working together emerged. The Church ceased to be a minority illegal faith. It ceased to be on the receiving end of state violence because it was now at the controlling end of the state machinery. This was wholly new and was not in the original blueprint of the Church. In scientific jargon, a foreign gene had been spliced into the original genetic code of the church creating a new hybrid which turned out to be a monster. When religion and politics go hand in hand, what results is a monolithic totalitarian system that will murder to enforce its will. That was why, in the Old Testament, the function of king and priest were separated in Israel. The other religions had their king and priest together in the one person.

In 313 the Edict of Milan was issued giving full legal toleration of Christianity. The physical battle for the Church ended but other new battles more detrimental to its life began. The Church enjoyed increasing favour under Constantine's patronage with restitution of confiscated property, financial aid for the Church, clerical exemption for hereditary offices and civil jurisdiction for bishops. Christianity became the official state religion and gained respectability.

Constantine found the Church in a bad state as the Arian controversy raged. He called some 300 bishops to Nicea for a Council to resolve this controversy. Constantine's ambitions for a church-wide attendance were disappointed. The Council was dominated by bishops from the Eastern Church, with only four or five bishops from the West. Bishop Sylvester of Rome was represented by two presbyters. The lame and the maimed survivors of the persecution came. Athanasius, the main opponent of Arius, was "only a deacon" and too young to be allowed into the Council. He was however able to feed his arguments to friends on the inside. The Council of Nicea in the end adopted the creed of Eusebius of Caesarea's church as a base, with additional parts, to deal with the Arian heresy. The word *homoousios* meaning "same substance" was included to declare belief in the divinity of Christ. Most of the bishops signed, though some with reluctance.

It was apparent that this unity was paper-thin. Constantine, while seeking harmony, had no theological insight and was increasing influenced by a close friend of Arius, Eusebius of Nicomedia. He exiled Athanasius, who had to flee for his life five times over this controversy. Despite this Athanasius continued to fight the battle. For the first time then, civil power was used to resolve theological matters. While many would agree with the outcome, this was, nevertheless, a dangerous precedent. Civil sanctions would now increasingly be used to enforce ecclesiastical censures.

The Council of Nicea also issued 20 "canons" regulating various aspect of church life, including readmission of penitent splinter groups, and functions and business activities of deacons and clergy. Other canons strengthened the government of the Church into provinces and recognised that the bishops of Rome, Alexandria, Antioch, Caesarea and Jerusalem had superior authority. The four bishops in the East were soon joined by Constantinople. The basis for the future carving-up of the Church into the five patriarchates of Rome, Constantinople, Antioch, Jerusalem and Alexandria were thus laid.

In 330, Constantine set up his capital in Constantinople, located for strategic and Christian reasons far from old Rome, symbol of the pagan past. However, this move gave rise to the growing importance and power of the Western bishops, especially of Rome.

Constantine was baptised shortly before he died by Eusebius of Nicomedia because it was taught that after baptism one could not indulge in sin. He therefore "wisely" left it until the point of death before asking for baptism. There is no mention of genuine repentance and scholars are divided over the authenticity of his faith. Was it faith or superstition? He was buried in the basilica he had built in Constantinople to house his treasure of religious relics. Constantine and his mother, Helena, were keen patrons of church buildings and religious relics. Numerous buildings were created by them to house these relics and images. The tradition of relics and buildings may be traced to this period of history.

* * * * * * * * * * * *

As we look at the end of the first 400 years of church history, we see that the Church had indeed conquered the world. It has been estimated that some 5 per cent of the Roman Empire were Christians by the time of Constantine. This is a growth of half a million per generation. From Constantine to Theodosius I's enforcement of Christianity, the number of Christians rose from 5 per cent to around 50 per cent of the imperial populace (Ramsay MacMullen, *Christianizing the Roman Empire*). The Christians had won because they had outlived, out-thought and out-died all others. And yet all was not what it seems. The quality of some of this growth is suspect. Did Jesus ever intend the Church to be like this? The nature of the Church and its testimony were becoming less and less distinctive. Had the Church really conquered the world or had the world in fact seduced it into a false sense of triumph?

4

HOW THE WORLD
CONQUERED THE CHURCH

(AD 400 - 1400)

The Church has been described as a lifeboat to save souls. A lifeboat has to be in the sea to respond to the SOS distress calls. But if the sea gets into the lifeboat, it is finished. In the same way, the church declines when the world finds its way in. If the first 400 years has been called "How the Church conquered the world", the next 1,000 years sees the Church being conquered by the world.

Satan had failed to destroy the Church over the first 300 years through violent persecution. Instead of extinction, the Church actually thrived during this period of persecution. This was a lesson he should have learnt from the Israelites in Egypt. The more they were persecuted, the more they multiplied (Ex. 1:12). A change of tactic was called for. He now sought to destroy the Church through assimilation. If the Church cannot be eliminated, it can be infiltrated and assimilated by the world: perversion rather than persecution. Either way, Satan's objective - to render the Church impotent - would be achieved. Governments that are either hostile or overly friendly towards the Church are equally dangerous to its survival. Let us turn now to look at some of the changes that took place in the post-Constantinian era. What kind of a Church was it? Can the Church maintain its faithfulness to the Lord given its new respectability in the eyes of the Emperor? How will the Church relate to this new friendly imperial power? This was a special relationship, unique in the history of the Church. Will this "marriage" work or will it lead to tears? We shall examine a number of issues where the Church during this period departed from its New Testament model to become more and more like the world.

1. Church government

This period saw the further establishment of the metropolitan bishops, leading eventually to the setting up of the patriarchal system. As we saw earlier, the New Testament model was that every church had several bishops or elders who cared for the flock and were responsible to Christ as Head. This plurality gave way in the Early Church to a situation where each church was reduced to having only one bishop. Eventually, the model was that of several churches in each city sharing a bishop. By Ignatius' time (d.115), churches in Asia Minor were already ruled by the "threefold ministry". This consisted of a single bishop, a group of presbyters (priests) and deacons (regarded as pre-presbyters). Ignatius was a pioneer of this kind of "monarchical episcopacy". However, it was not until the second half of the second century that Rome adopted this structure of a single bishop and other places developed even more slowly. There was generally, however, an established pattern of a single bishop per city before Constantine. What developed after Constantine was the pattern of the bishop as area ecclesiastical administrator. Leadership was increasingly concentrated in fewer and fewer hands. These developments laid the foundation for the eventual basis of the papacy.

Before the Constantinian era, bishops were elected by their congregations to teach and pastor the flock. They dressed and lived no differently from the other members of the Church and their only source of financial support was the congregation. Things changed during Constantine's reign. The clergy were entertained at the emperor's table and became his travelling companions and counsellors. Churchmen owned slaves, raised their own armies, and sought power and wealth - laying the foundation for the papal state. Further authority was conferred on the bishops at the Council of Nicea during which the bishops of Rome, Antioch, Jerusalem and Alexandria were accorded the title Patriarch. After the founding of Constantinople as the imperial capital in 334, the bishop of Rome acquired even more authority, permitting him to preside over the bishops of Antioch and Alexandria. The bishopric of Rome thus became a prestigious position, carrying both power and wealth. The Roman historian Ammianus, commenting on the lifestyle of the Roman clergy, described them as "riding in carriages, dressing splendidly and feasting luxuriously so that their entertainment surpasses even the royal banquet". This was a position worth fighting for and was open to abuse by unscrupulous social climbers. During the reign of Valentinian (364-67), a dispute over the election of the bishop of Rome ended in a bloody battle between the followers of Damasus and Ursinus.

In a short period after the death of the apostles, when churches were founded from Palestine to Rome, a clerical and hierarchical system of church government had become established. There were a number of reasons for this development:

1) The emergence of false teaching such as Gnosticism, Docetism, Arianism and Manichaeism led to the emergence of charismatic leaders in the Church who championed the truth. These able teachers and apologists were respected and soon had conferred on them an authority that even Peter or Paul never had.

2) There was also a feeling of safety in numbers because of the persecution. Therefore one bishop began to have oversight over a number of churches in an area. As we have seen, the term "bishop" in the New Testament was used interchangeably with "elder". From the time of the Early Church onwards, the bishop became the "overseer" and the presbyter was the local elder. This was a new differentiation not seen in the New Testament. The name bishop was gradually changed from that of a function to that of an office with authority. Clericalism had evolved.

3) The imitation of the government of the world followed. Just as Israel wanted a king "like the other nations" (1Sam. 8:5), the

Church could not live with only Jesus as King but needed a structure of government like the world's. So churches were divided into regions, and bishops of important political cities and regions were also the most powerful and influential in the Church. The model that was adopted was in essence that of the Roman Empire

Bishops of churches exercised dominion over an administrative district parallel to the civil administration of the Empire.

This distinction between clergy and laity, which was already developing in the late second century, became more and more defined, resulting in some further aberrations. The priesthood of believers had somehow been forgotten and a new class of professionally trained clergy was created who could read, chant, administer the sacraments and govern the institution. For this they were to be given privileges for their services to God and country. This status quo was assisted by the decline in literacy as the Empire collapsed in the sixth century. The uneducated laity unable to read the Bible became more and more dependent on the clergy in matters of creed and conduct. As Rome was the centre of the Empire, Latin was adopted as the "spiritual" language in which the Bible was read and the Mass conducted. No vernacular language was allowed for the Bible or the Mass.

2. Magical view of sacraments

Views on baptism changed during this period too. The water and the use of the right formula were believed of themselves to save a person. Salvation was no longer by faith through the sacraments. Instead, partaking of the sacraments alone could save. The Church had also started to teach that one could not sin after baptism without losing its benefit. Many therefore chose to be baptised on their death beds. This was called "Clinical Baptism" (Gk *kline* meaning bed). Others asked about babies who died, and the practice of paedo-baptism was started some 150 years after Christ.

The first clear reference to infant baptism is in a writing of Tertullian in 197, in which he condemned the introduction of the practice of baptising the dead and infants. The whole issue of infant baptism was to play a critical part in the unfolding drama of the Church. It was an instrument that would be seized on by the civil government for its own advantage and would become the major test of "orthodoxy". The biblical justification for paedo-baptism was provided by Augustine of Hippo, to whom we shall turn later. An equally striking change was the doctrine of transubstantiation. In this, the bread and the wine at the Lord's Supper were "miraculously changed" into the actual body and blood of Jesus when administered by the priests. This only served to increase superstition within the Church and intensified the growing distinction between clergy and laity. The simple Lord's Supper was transformed with pomp and ceremony into the Mass - yet more magic to impress and suppress the common people.

3. Sacerdotalism

Associated with this view was an important and fundamental shift in the doctrine of salvation. The Church now taught that salvation could only be found in the Church and by means of its sacraments administered by its priests. Sacerdotalism became a powerful tool in the hands of the bishops. In 390, there was a riot in a Greek city over the imprisonment of a popular charioteer. The "Christian" Emperor Theodosius ordered a bloody massacre lasting three hours which resulted in more than 5,000 killed. Bishop Ambrose of Milan was so angered by this that he bravely refused Theodosius the sacraments until he had publicly humbled himself several times as a sign of repentance. This was a brave and noble act by Ambrose but it showed that sacerdotalism was now the ultimate weapon that could bring even the all-powerful emperor to heel. The threat of excommunication and therefore eternal damnation was one that the Church would repeatedly use for its own ends. This event also showed the increasing power and influence of the Church over the State.

4. Established religion

The emperor went to church, therefore it became fashionable for everyone to follow. An established religion tends to produce a fashionable and respectable Christianity devoid of life, power and authenticity. Nominal membership became the norm because the Church had become an institution. The growth of the Church may have been even faster than in the first three hundred years, but most of this was nominal in nature. Until the sixth or eighth century, baptism was often delayed, depending on the area of the Empire. Many people rarely attended church even though they were "Christians".

Sunday was introduced as a day of rest in 321 by Constantine. Christians were exempt from civil and army duties to attend church on Sundays, adding to the attraction of Christianity. This was only one of the many policies of "positive discrimination" introduced by Constantine for Christians.

5. Pagan customs

Roman temples were commandeered and used as places of worship for the Christians. The early Christians had no special buildings, but met in private houses. The earliest known church building is generally thought to be at Dura-Europos, Syria where a house dating from 232 was used for about 100 people to assemble. In Rome, about 18 churches still bear the name of their early owner or patron, with origins before Constantine. Without exception, these early church buildings were small and simple. After Constantine, the picture changed completely as large and impressive building were erected in many places. Imperial funds were made available for the building of churches, including St Peter's Basilica in Rome and the Church of the Holy Sepulchre in Jerusalem.

The church took over other pagan ideas and images. From sun worship came the celebration of Christ's birthday on December 25, the birthday of the sun. Saturnalia, the Roman winter festival of December 17-21, provided the gift-giving and candles later to be adopted by the Church, as were the vestments of the Roman priests. Later, the use of incense was also "Christianised" and brought into the Church. Constantine was viewed as God's chosen servant to express Christ's rule on the earth. The reverence for Constantine can be seen in Byzantine art in which Christ enthroned in heaven looks suspiciously like Constantine.

The veneration of the Virgin Mary was probably stimulated by parallels in pagan religion. Some scholars believe that the worship of Artemis (Diana) of Ephesus or Isis, the Egyptian goddess, was transferred to Mary. The cult of saints and martyrs grew rapidly in the fourth century. Chapels and churches began to be built over the tombs of martyrs, a practice that influenced church architecture. Competition for saintly corpses became intense and degenerated into a superstitious search for relics. This practice was approved and encouraged by the great Christian leaders of the age, including Jerome, Ambrose and Augustine. It was boasted that in many places saints and martyrs took the place of pagan gods, and their shrines the place of pagan temples. Such superstitions led Vigilantius, an obscure priest from Aquitaine, to write:

"We almost see the rites of the pagans introduced into the Church under the pretext of religion; ranks of candles are lit in full daylight; and everywhere people kiss and adore some bit of dust in a little pot, wrapped in a precious fabric."

The strong pagan influences changed Christianity in the fourth century into a new Christianised pagan cult.

6. Christian sacralism

By the time of Constantine and towards the end of the fourth century, Church and State had become fused together. The Church now had a political, civil and military arm to enforce its decrees. It was not long before it used its new found power. Furthermore, all those born and christened into the State would automatically be born into the Church and would therefore be "Christians".

The Roman Emperor, as head of the state religion, had the historical role of maintaining good relations between the people and the gods. Constantine naturally saw himself in a similar role as the Christian Emperor and was unafraid to intervene in matters of doctrines and church practice, as was seen by his role in the Council of Nicea and his intervention in the Donatist controversy (see page 95). Although some Christian leaders had originally accepted the Emperor's interference, others such as bishop Donatus, Athanasius and Ossius of Cardova, who had shaped Constantine's policy towards the Church, later rejected this role. The famous question of Donatus on this matter was "What has the Emperor to do with the Church?" The climax of imperial intervention came during the reign of Constantius, his son. During a dispute over the condemnation of Athanasius, the recommendation of the bishops to consult the canons of the Church was met with a strong reply from Constantius: "Whatever I will shall be regarded as a canon." Game, set and match! The emperor had assumed for himself the authority for formulating the canon laws that regulate the life of the church.

There was yet another aspect to this new "Christian sacralism". The word sacral means sanctified or made sacred. It can also mean "fused together" as in the sacral vertebrae of the spine. A sacral society is one in which the Church and the State are fused together, totally identified with and mutually reinforcing each other. Constantine and his son, Constantius, tolerated paganism within the Empire. However, during the reigns of Gratian and Theodosius I (379-95), the pagan religions were actively suppressed and outlawed. Gratian, under the influence of Ambrose, removed the altar of Victory from the Senate House in Rome, confiscated the revenues of the Vestal Virgins and other Roman priesthoods, and refused the title Pontifex Maximus (High Priest), which previous Emperors had taken (used by the Pope still). Theodosius in 381 and 385 prohibited sacrifices, destroyed temples or turned them into churches and finally banned private pagan worship. Sacralism is by definition intolerant of other expressions of faith. Homogeneity was the norm.

We shall consider this issue of sacralism which was to shape the rest of history in more detail when we consider the "Lessons from Church History".

* * * * * * * * * * *

The Church around 400 had ceased to be evangelical in its doctrine and practice. Salvation was seen to be centred on the sacraments and belonging to the Church. Traditions and especially the state machinery, took priority over the Bible in determining church structure. Evangelism had effectively ceased. It was almost as if the Church breathed a sigh of relief now that the persecutions were over and the Emperor was "one of us", and began to slip into a deep slumber. The impetus for growth had disappeared. The Church was now established and was clearly and visibly a part of the establishment. It had a large state institution to run and maintain. As a result, the Church was no longer pentecostal in its expression. Without ongoing evangelism, there was no need for the supernatural gifts. The presence of God with demonstrations of power were no longer needed. All institutions have a life of their own - the Church now had no need for the life of God. If anything God could become a great inconvenience in the new order. It was easier to govern the Church without the unpredictable nature of the Holy Spirit. The Church wanted order in its service and found the Spirit to be too disruptive.

Gone too was the radical emphasis of the Early Church. The Church as a respectable and increasingly domineering part of the establishment had no time for radical living which would strike at the very heart of the establishment. It was unthinkable that the Church would "kill the goose" that had given it this new found prominence and role in society. Even in the area of the sacramental, this period saw the Church with an increasingly superstitious attitude towards the sacraments. This was yet another case of corrupting the things of God when violent persecution had failed to destroy it. The Church then, within a period of 100 years post-Constantine, had become institutional. The seeds of later distortions were all sown during this period. Constantine may have introduced Christendom to the world. It was Augustine however who provided the "theological" justifications for many of these distortions.

The Church had been lured into trading in its authentic Christianity for a Christianised cult resembling Roman paganism. Like Jacob, the Church had sold its birthright for a bowl of stew (Gen. 25:29ff). It had mortgaged its future for some temporal benefits.

5

PROTEST MOVEMENTS
OF THE FIRST 400 YEARS

As the Church increased in number and became part of the establishment, its early zeal and witness flagged and conformity to the world increased. The decline of the Church in spirituality, its departure from the New Testament pattern, its growing worldliness and superstitions, and its partnership with the State did not, however, come about without protest. It is easy to have an erroneous impression that in the first three centuries there was one united Catholic Church with some unimportant heretical groups. On the contrary, there were, then as now, a number of significant divergent lines of testimony each marked by some special characteristics. These protest movements are a clear testimony that in every generation God has not left himself without a clear witness. From these protest movements have come groups that have kept the true faith alive, contributing to the recovery of truth even to this day.

One of the distinctive patterns in church history is the cycle of renewal : God begins a work, it grows, it becomes institutionalised, it declines, then faces protest and the cycle repeats itself. We will turn now to look at these protest movements. Just before we do, a number of qualifying remarks about them are necessary:

1) As has been noted, history is the propaganda of the victor. Whoever wins, writes history their way. Much of what we

know about the radical groups comes from the writings of their enemies. Some judgement must therefore be exercised and their testimony and writings compared with those of the persecuted. All were called "heretics" as a blanket term with which they could be legally and savagely persecuted in the name of the Church, whether Catholic or Protestant.

2) By view of their being protest movements, they were often isolated, ostracised and persecuted. These conditions have a tendency to cultivate some extreme views and practices in some groups. One should not, however, reject the validity of their witness because of their occasional excesses. The lives and testimony of these believers should speak for themselves.

The Early Church also suffered from such false accusations. Believers were rumoured to be cannibals eating human bodies and drinking human blood, a clear reference to the Lord's Supper. They were also accused of practising sexual orgies because of their regular "love feasts." They were called "atheists" because they refused to worship idols.

Montanists (mid 2nd Century)

The Montanist movement was started by Montanus in Phrygia (Asia Minor). It later spread to North Africa where it was most influential. The followers of Montanus initially worked for reform within the Catholic Church, protesting against its increasing worldliness and formalism. It remained as an underground protest movement for decades, often in very humble and obscure settings. They were one of the earliest groups that attempted to return to a simple apostolic faith.

The Montanists emphasised a return to primitive piety, local government of churches, gifts of the Holy Spirit and eschatology (doctrine of the last things or end time). They sought to revive the deadness of the established Church through the restoration of the work of the Holy Spirit. It was the charismatic renewal movement of the second and third century. Montanism was a powerful movement and came close to persuading the whole Church that what they stood for was authentic biblical Christianity. Had they done so, church history would have been different. There was also an emphasis on Body life and ministry which was open to all including women. Two women in particular, Prisca and Maxmilla, were leading prophetesses. Tertullian was one of the leading members of this movement. He was a prolific writer, an eloquent preacher and one of the leading Early Church fathers.

The Montanists, however, eventually went into error with exaggerations of spiritual revelations and the imminent return of the Lord. There were elements of extremism and fanaticism. They had elevated the gifts of revelation above the inspirational Word of the Bible. It was akin to a speedboat without a rudder; the Corinthian church without the discipline of a Paul. In its later history, there was no one of the calibre of Tertullian to guide the movement. It was a valid reaction against the established Church of its day but in the process they over-reacted and swung the pendulum too far. This is always a danger of protest movements. Satan's strategy to keep the Church from exercising the power and gifts of the Spirit had succeeded with the established Church. The Montanists posed a new threat to Satan and the way to neutralise them was to push them into extremism, so bringing discredit to the whole issue of the supernatural gifts. As we look at the history of the mainstream churches, we cannot but acknowledge that this strategy has largely been successful. Robbed of the power and gifts of the Spirit, the Church was made impotent for many centuries until the beginning of the twentieth century when the Pentecostal Movement restored them to the Church.

Monasticism

Alongside the protests of the Montanists, some began to withdraw themselves from society to seek holiness and communion with God. Influenced by Platonic teachings that the material world and sexual activity were evil, they adopted a simple and ascetic lifestyle to overcome the flesh.

In the fourth century, Antony of Egypt became celebrated for his solitary life. He inspired many to withdraw into the desert with him and laid down simple rules for their lives as hermits. It should be noted that the radical living of the early centuries was now associated with monks who were often charismatics. Antony was a great charismatic figure, always fighting demons. The "desert fathers" were intensely spiritual people who provided spiritual wisdom to many; people today continue to draw from their insights. Later in the sixth century, Benedict of Nursia in Italy started the Benedictine monastic movement. The Benedictine monasteries emphasised serving others rather than focusing on personal spirituality alone. It was a great missionary movement spreading to Germany, Ireland and Scotland. Not only was there a radical dimension to their lives, the monastics also took on the responsibility of mission.

The monastic movement was a valid protest against the state of the Church. It sought to call the Church back to holy living. However for them, holy living meant asceticism and withdrawal from the world. Jesus, however, calls us to live holy lives in the world. This call to holy living needs to be heeded by the Church today. The monastics also called the Church back to a radical lifestyle of serving and giving to the poor and needy. The Fransciscan movement is one such that should challenge us today. The various monastic orders all followed one course of development, however. Beginning with poverty and severe self-denial, they eventually became rich and powerful as land and properties were donated to them. As they became established and institutionalised, they relaxed their discipline and grew in self-indulgence and worldliness. They became indistinguishable in spirit from the Catholic Church. Then a reform or protest would be sparked - as with reformers such as Bernard of Clairvaux and Francis of Assisi - and a new order of absolute self-humiliation would start and the cycle repeated itself.

Novatians (3rd Century)

The Novatians was a name given to protest groups who claimed an unbroken apostolic succession of testimony. Novatian of Rome was not the founder of the movement but one of its most prominent leaders after whom it was named. He was a gifted theologian and wrote the first full-length treatment on the Trinity which championed true Christology. He is also renowned as the "anti-pope" candidate of the "Puritan" party in the Church in opposition to Cornelius who was supported by Cyprian. Novatian died a martyr during the Valerian persecution.

The Novatians laid special emphasis on piety and purity. They stood firm regarding the controversy over readmission of those who had "lapsed" (offered to idols since their baptism) or who had apostasised during the Decian persecutions (249-50). The Novatians would not receive such people back into the Church. It was not easy for those who had remained faithful during the persecution to welcome back leaders who had given up the Scriptures to be burned and recanted their faith.

The Novatians were officially excommunicated by the synod at Rome in 251 and separated from the Catholic Church. They were certainly orthodox in their doctrines as evidenced by their strong opposition to Arianism. In their practice, however, they were radical in seeking to return to New Testament principles of church life.

Donatists (4th Century)

The Donatists were a North African separatist church movement under the able leadership of Donatus (d.355) and Parmenian (355-91). The initial cause of the Donatist schism was the appointment of a new Bishop of Carthage who had compromised his faith during the Diocletion persecution by surrendering copies of the Scriptures. The Donatists did not accept him (or any clergy ordained by him and his successors) and set up a breakaway church. In this respect there is a similarity with the Novation schism. They protested eventually however against the new Christian sacralism of the Constantinian church. They attempted to conserve the concept of the Church as a voluntary gathering "based on personal faith". They stood in the line of Cyprian and Tertullian in demanding a pure church of the martyrs as opposed to a state-church.

The Donatists emphasised believers' baptism or "re-baptisms" for those who had been baptised as infants. They also taught and practised rigorous piety, held a puritan ecclesiology, adulated martyrs and rejected the union of Church and State. They emphasised the character of those who administered the sacraments, while the Catholics considered the sacraments themselves as more important. In all this, they acknowledged the influence of Tertullian and Novatian who preceded them.

In parts of North Africa, they became the dominant group of Christians. Only later, during the era of Augustine and Aurelius, Bishop of Carthage (391-430), did the Catholics increase, but not without imperial coercion in the Edict of Unity (405) and other decrees proscribing Donatism. Emperor Constantine, together with some of the bishops, started persecuting the Donatists of North Africa from 316. They were only completely blotted out by the Muslims in the seventh century.

Priscillians

The Priscillians were named after their founder Priscillian, a wealthy Spaniard convert and energetic reformer within the Catholic Church. He was regarded by all as a saintly man who was influential throughout Spain, France and even Rome.

The Priscillians practised an ascetic lifestyle in protest against the moral laxity within the Catholic Church. They emphasised salvation as a spiritual act, not magic brought about by sacraments. In this they repudiated sacerdotalism. They also emphasised piety, some evangelical doctrines, the work of the Holy Spirit and Bible study for laity as well as clergy. His followers showed some Gnostic tendencies although Priscillian himself may have been less extreme.

Priscillian became the Bishop of Avila but soon attracted the hostility of the Spanish clergy, who regarded him as an upstart rocking the boat. He and his followers were accused of witchcraft and immorality. Neither accusation was substantiated yet they were condemned to execution by the Church. Protests from eminent bishops such as Martin of Tours and Ambrose of Milan were to no avail. Priscillian and six of his followers were beheaded as heretics in 385.

This was a very significant event, a landmark in the history of the Church. This is the first instance of the execution of Christians by the Church. The persecuted had become the persecutor in less than 100 years. It was a tragic moment in church history heralding the start of many murders of Christians by Christians. The Church, having the civil and political power of the State by its side, soon used it on its enemies within the Church as well as outside. The Church perfected its means of persecution and execution into an art by applying it to countless thousands throughout the centuries. The signs of the true nature of the hybrid were becoming manifest and these early signs did not bode well for the future. How could the followers of the One who taught that his followers should love their enemies resort to murdering their fellow believers?

6

THE DARK AGES

(AD 400-1000)

In 410, catastrophe struck the Roman Empire in the form of the barbarian invasions. The Germanic tribes of Vandals, Goths, Angles, Saxons, Danes, Vikings and Normans - all of Europe's ferocious migrants - came from the north and attacked the Empire. The Goths sacked Rome in 410. The Vandals, after moving south through Spain, east along the north coast of Africa, and then briefly up into Italy, sacked the imperial city again in 455. Roman soldiers stationed in Britain returned to Rome to defend it. The Anglo-Saxons took advantage and conquered Britain.

The fall of Rome and the collapse of the Roman Empire was a profound shock for everyone. Jerome of Rome said: "The human race was included in the ruin." There was much soul searching as a result. How was it that pagan Rome had withstood attacks for so many centuries and yet "Christian" Rome had fallen? What had changed? The only thing that had changed as far as some were concerned was the adoption of Christianity. The god of the Christians could not defend Rome against the barbarians. The empire's new religion, Christianity, was therefore to blame.

This was a disturbing criticism and Augustine of Hippo took up his pen to argue the Christian case. He wrote his second book,

The City of God, in which he said that the fall of Rome was unimportant because it was an earthly city. All that mattered was the city of God which would never fall because its citizens were immortal. According to Augustine, the fall of Rome had enabled the heavenly empire to come into being.

With the fall of the Roman Empire, the Church with its considerable influence rose to fill this new political vacuum. The Bishop of Rome assumed the role of emperor. There was great debate about the name Pope (meaning "Father") but the papacy was finally and firmly established. The pope adopted the title Pontifex Maximus (High Priest), the title and robes of the Roman emperor so that people thought that the Church was the new empire, the Kingdom of God with all the trappings of pope-emperor, robes and ceremonies. This was a completely new view of the Church. Augustine viewed the Church entering a golden age and building Christendom on earth.

The Celtic churches of France, Ireland and Scotland were not prepared to accept these changes. The monasteries founded by St Columba and his followers from their base on the island of Iona, in western Scotland, practised a form of Celtic Christianity whereas Augustine of Canterbury (not the same as Augustine of Hippo) established papal Christianity which came to dominate Britain after an agreement in Whitby, England, in 664. From then on the spirituality and missionary zeal of the Celtic Church was merged with the organised and sophisticated papal church. The British Isles came under papal control.

However, the churches of the East, Syria, Greece and Asia Minor did not agree with these changes. They split with the Church of Rome to form the Orthodox Churches of the East. This rift was gradual but was finally completed in 1054. The reasons for this break up are complicated. It was a mixture of doctrines, personalities and jealousy over primacy of each regional church. Not until the 1960s did the Roman and Orthodox churches re-establish formal relationships though they continue to be separate and mutually suspicious.

Leo I (the Great) was Pope from 440. He advanced the primacy of the Roman church in the West and was the first bishop of Rome to make extensive use of the text "You are Peter" (Matt. 16:19) for himself. His claim to be the successor of the Apostle Peter was based on a decretal or papal letter (of which there were many with the same papal authority) stating that Peter was appointed the first Pope and Leo the second. This was quite a claim! There were many links between Peter and Leo but many of the early ones are mere names which cannot be checked. In 850 the letter was shown to be an obvious and blatant forgery. This was the background to the creation of the papacy.

Another notable forgery was the *Donation of Constantine*, a document supposedly written by him giving Rome and the western region of the empire to Pope Sylvester I. Constantine probably gave the Lateran palace to the Church of Rome after 321, when it could legally own property; but that was all. By 660, gifts of large estate formed the Patrimony of Peter around which grew the legend that Constantine had donated these lands to the Papacy I. From 756 to 1870, certain civil territories in Italy acknowledged the Pope as their temporal ruler. The Vatican does to this day.

Pope Gregory I (590) was the main person responsible for strengthening the position of the Pope. He maintained that the See of Peter had been entrusted with the care of the entire Church and therefore had universal jurisdiction. He reversed a decision made by the patriarch of Constantinople (John IV the Faster) against two priests and strongly objected to the patriarch's use of the title "ecumenical (universal) bishop". He is regarded as one of the four great doctors of the Roman Catholic Church in moral theology and was a prolific writer.

Throughout this period, the Pope functioned as a kind of "emperor" of the former Roman Empire with power in the East and West. The Church in effect ruled the State and all the princes were subject to the Pope. This was a time of immense worldly power and influence for the Church, which amassed properties and wealth on a grand scale.

Then something happened which at once enhanced and curtailed the influence of the Church. In 742, a man was born who had a dream that the Roman Empire should be put back on the map with Rome as the capital but with the Pope under him. His name was Charles, later to be changed to Charlemagne, the King of the Franks. From 771 onwards, he spent 30 years in warfare. His most notable victory was the conquest of the Saxons gained through massacres, forced conversion, mass deportation, and organising Saxony into counties and dioceses under the rule of the Franks. He defeated the Lombards and annexed northern Italy in 774. He crushed the Bavarian and heathen Slavs, opening the way for the German colonisation of Eastern Europe. Charlemagne was credited with saving the life of Pope Leo III on two occasions - once from barbarians, the other from angry crowds. In gratitude for this, Charlemagne was crowned the Holy Roman Emperor by Pope Leo III on December 25 AD800 in the largest church in Rome. History had completed a cycle. When the Empire had fallen in 410, the Church took control of the Empire. Now the Empire had taken over the Church. As this challenged the Byzantine emperors (who regarded themselves as Constantine's successors, and saw Charlamegne's new status as a challenge to these claims), Charlemagne worked to improve relations with the East.

Charlemagne carried out some good and much needed reforms in the Church. He cleaned up the morals of the clergy by prohibiting them from having concubines, going hunting and visiting taverns. These prohibitions give an indication of the state of the Church. He also started many schools. But he also left some bad legacies. He recognised the celibacy of the priesthood and coined the phrase "Christendom", an earthly kingdom which will be Christ's kingdom. He saw the Pope and himself as partners with him as the senior. Charlemagne undoubtedly strengthened the Church through unifying Europe. The Church by this stage was wealthy, worldly and powerful. It was corrupt, worshipped images, sold indulgences and made pilgrimages to earn salvation.

In the East, a storm was brewing in the form of Islam. Muhammad was born in 571 in Mecca, the centre of idolatrous practices in Arabia. He turned first to the Jews and then to Christians for an answer. The tragedy was that he never met a true Christian. All he saw were crucifixes, images, priests, vestments. Christianity was as idolatrous as the Arabian religions. Repulsed by all the idolatry, he set out to establish a pure religion. He married a wealthy widow and in the desert he received the revelation of the Koran and became the prophet of the new religion. Persecutions led him to flee to Medina in 622 but he returned with an army and imposed his religion by force. The rise of Islam through conquest by Arab armies swept Christianity out of North Africa, Palestine, Spain, France (up to Lyon) and Eastern Europe as far as Vienna. Christianity vanished from most of these areas. Islam has been said to be the greatest judgement God has ever allowed on the Church. Islam is a sacral religion which drew its doctrines from both Judaism and Christianity but regards Muhammad as the final prophet. Its predestination and fatalism, as well as its use of conversion by coercion, come from the sacral view of society that was prevalent in his day. He only had to look at the behaviour of the Church or the teachings of Augustine to learn about these things, had he cared to.

7

THE AUGUSTINIAN CHANGE

We said earlier that Constantine was an enigma. The same can be said of Augustine of Hippo. Where Constantine brought about structural changes to the Church's organisation, Augustine sowed the seeds of significant theological changes to its teachings. Both are equally destructive. The nature of the Church and its teachings affect our view of God. Augustine provided much of the theological justifications for the Constantinian change. Augustine of Hippo has possibly had more influence on church history than any other man - both good and bad.

So who was he? Augustine was born in North Africa and studied rhetoric in Carthage. He had a brilliant mind but was influenced by Manichaeism and lived a loose life. He had a son by a concubine. He became a teacher of rhetoric in Milan where he heard the preaching of Ambrose which was instrumental in his conversion long prayed for by his godly mother, Monica. His book Confessions was his testimony of how he found Christ.

Augustine's theology was formulated largely in response to three situations - the disputes with the Donatists and Pelagius and the fall of the Roman Empire. Let us turn firstly to his disputes with the Donatists. As we had seen earlier, the Donatists wanted a "pure" Church of true believers. They rejected Catholic baptism and the union of Church and State which they believed would lead to nominalism. They attacked the growing corruption of the clergy and argued that moral character was important in those administering the sacraments. All these, as we have argued, were New Testament and Early Church beliefs. Augustine responded to the Donatist schism by teaching that the church's holiness was not related to that of its members but of its head, Christ. He differentiated between the "invisible" and the "visible" Church. It did not matter that the visible local church was corrupt and "impure"; what was important was the purity of the invisible Church. He played down the importance of faithfulness and discipleship to Christ. Grace was emphasised but "works" neglected. Furthermore, he taught that Christ was the real minister of the sacraments. Therefore the validity of baptism and the Eucharist was unaffected by the moral character of the human agent. As long as he was of the Church clergy, the sacraments were valid. In reality it was the sacraments administered by the Church which saved.

It was this kind of teaching that enhanced the doctrine of sacerdotalism (salvation by the Church through its sacraments), which was already developed by Augustine's time. In his controversy with Pelagius, Augustine formulated his teachings about infant baptism, original sin and predestination. He based his teachings on infant or paedo-baptism on the concept of original guilt. Augustine argued that each child is not only born with an inherited tendency towards sin, but also shares in the guilt of Adam. It is noteworthy that Augustine based this position largely on the faulty text of Rom. 5:12 - a Latin version which translated the Greek phrase eph ho (meaning "because that") as "in quo" (meaning "in whom") all sinned. On the basis of this faulty text, Augustine taught that all mankind was bound up in Adam and all sinned in Adam. He extended the concept of original sin which was passed down from parents to children by teaching that the locus of its transmission was sexual intercourse. Baptism was indispensable for salvation because of the original sin present. All infants dying unbaptised would therefore be condemned to hell. Augustine did not suggest that infants had faith but that the faith of the Church was of benefit to them. This remains a classic position for justifying infant baptism. In all this we see the influence of

Platonic dualism in his thinking - this separation between the visible and invisible, grace and works, between the physical and the spiritual. This dualism has, for instance, shaped the Church's attitude towards sex for centuries. Whereas the Hebrew did not differentiate between the sacred and the secular and had a whole book in the Old Testament, Song of Solomon, in praise of the love between a man and a woman, Augustine regarded physical love as something "sinful". This has come ultimately from Greek thought.

He further opposed Pelagius' teaching about free will. Augustine taught that man was so bound up in sin that God's irresistible grace was required to free the will so that we can turn to Him. This grace was not for all, only for a "fixed number of the elect". He denied that God wants all persons to be saved. He formulated a doctrine of predestination which is for the elect, leaving the rest of mankind condemned. Augustine clearly did not believe that "God so loved the world ". It seems that Augustine's God only loved the "elect," ie those predestined for salvation. Scholars, in defence of Augustine, have "credited" Gottschalk, an Augustinian in the ninth century, with the doctrine of "double predestination", that is, the predestination of some to heaven and others to hell. This is purely cosmetic! While Augustine may not have directly taught "double predestination", this was clearly implied in his teaching. What kind of God have we here?

The logical next step from this view of predestination is what theologians call "the infallibility of the eternal redemption of the elect"! Translated, this means that once saved, the elect cannot lose salvation. This is the logical conclusion if the elect have been predestined and cannot resist God's grace. This kind of teaching does not take into account that the New Testament speaks about salvation as a continuous process - we have been saved, we are being saved and we will be saved. We are to go on believing (John 3:16f), keep on working out our salvation (Phil. 2:12). It also ignores the strong warnings of the Bible about being unfaithful (Heb. 6:4ff) and the book of Revelation which speaks about "overcomers". This kind of teaching makes for complacent believers. Those "elect" who know they have been saved can live as they please - which was precisely what they did in the medieval Church.[1]

[1] Readers should be aware that my conclusions on Augustine are 'radical'. For a detailed treatment of these issues, see *God's Strategy in Human History* by Roger T. Forster & V. Paul Marston, Tyndale House Publishers.

We turn next to Augustine's concept of Church and State. He saw history as the struggle between the City of God and the Earthly City. With the collapse of Rome, the heavenly city became even more important. While this heavenly city can only be fully manifested in the future, nevertheless Augustine and his subsequent followers saw a place for its outworking on earth through the Church/State partnership. The common concept of the time was to view history in seven day-ages. The Church era is the sixth day, immediately before the eternal sabbath. It is the millennium of Rev. 20:6. Certainly as the Church increased in power and wealth throughout the Middle Ages, it appeared as if Christendom was experiencing the millennial reign of Christ. Even if Augustine himself did not articulate a theocracy of the Church, his followers understood him in this way. For them the Kingdom of God had come on earth. If this is true, it must therefore be right to use the powers of the State for the good of the Kingdom. In this context, conversion by coercion is justifiable - as indeed was taught by Augustine. He saw no difficulties about the Church having the sword of the State in one hand and the sword of the Spirit in the other. It was for their own good that people should be made to become Christians! The Church as an earthly kingdom had the power of the State to enforce conversion.

In this context, Augustine was also able to present the most substantial argument to date for the "Just War". Eusebius in his *Church History* (4th century) had written about Constantine's campaigns as holy wars. Christians were no longer a minority and the growth of the Church made it difficult to maintain pacifism. Combining the Old Testament with ideas from Aristotle, Plato and Cicero, Augustine formulated a series of rules to regulate violence and permit believers to fight for the Empire. In fairness to Augustine, his grudging acceptance of war reflected a genuine respect for pacifism.

Protestants and Catholics have both appealed to Augustine's writings to support their creed as well as conduct. Augustine's genius, it seems, could be in appearing as "all things to all men". A case in point is the doctrine of transubstantiation. This teaching of the Eucharist was first defined by Radbertus in 831. However, his pupil, Ratramnus (d.ca. 868), emphasised a more symbolic interpretation which denied the "magical" view of the Eucharist. Both appealed to Augustine! His teachings, however, gave rise to unspeakable misery and sufferings caused by those who appealed to them. While the doctrine of sacerdotalism was already developed, it was Augustine who further defined and crystallised its theology in his teachings. He was also influential in formulating the doctrine of predestination, paedo-baptism and the use of coercion in conversion. His outward view of the Church as an earthly organisation led him to justify the use of earthly means for preserving and even forcing unity.

8

PROTEST MOVEMENTS

AD 400-1000

There were protest groups scattered all over Europe during the Dark Ages. These were groups of Christians who met around the Word in all simplicity. They saw that the official Church was increasingly corrupt and worldly. They believed that priests and popes were unnecessary because Jesus was their High Priest and God was their Papa (Father).

Paulicians (6th/7th Century)

The Paulicians were an evangelical group of churches predominantly in Armenia, Asia Minor, north Syria and Mesopotamia. Their roots date back to the apostolic churches. The apostle Paul planted churches in Asia Minor to which the Paulicians traced their origins.

They had a high view of the authority of the Scriptures (especially Luke and Paul but rejected the Old Testament, like Marcion) and regarded them as the basis of their creed and conduct. They rejected Mariolatry (worship of Mary), images and hagiolatry (worship of saints). They practised believers' baptism and were anti-hierarchical in their practice of church government. They were accused by their enemies of being dualists but they repudiated Manichaeism. The book *Key of Truth* was written by

95

an unknown Armenian author belonging to the Paulician church. In it are several instructions relating to church life: it states that repentance and faith should come first, then baptism - which should be carried out in rivers or other water in the open air; ordination of elders required careful consideration as character was important. These instructions give us an insight into what was happening with the official Church.

Constantine Sylvanus was one of the most prominent leaders of the movement. An Armenian by birth, Sylvanus laboured for 27 years in preaching the gospel before being stoned to death in 684. The Byzantine emperor, Constantine Pogonatus, had issued a decree banning the congregations. His persecutor Simone had ordered Sylvanus' personal friends to stone him but they refused. However, his adopted son, Justus, flung a stone at Sylvanus killing him. Simone was so moved by what he saw and heard that he was himself converted and became the successor to Sylvanus. Simone was himself later betrayed, again by Justus, and burnt as a heretic in 690.

The Paulician churches were protected by Emperor Constantine Copronymus (741-75), who was himself a Paulician. They increased in numbers during his reign. However, under Empress Theodora (842-57) there were savage persecutions of these churches and some 100,000 were martyred, leaving the Paulicians decimated and near to extinction. This was one of the greatest mass-murders of Christians by the official Church in the entire history of Christianity.

In response to the persecutions, the Paulicians organised armies which proved skilful in battle. The emperors moved them from their native Armenia to the Balkans (present-day Bulgaria) to defend the Empire against the Slavs and Bulgars. Scattered communities survived in Armenia, Asia Minor, and the Balkans where they may have merged with the Bogomiles, Cathari and Albigenses. The Crusaders found them everywhere in Syria and Palestine, and the Anabaptists were known to have contact with them.

Bogomiles (10th-11th Century)

The Bogomiles probably derived from the spread of the Paulicians. They became known as Bogomiles (meaning "Friends of God") in Bulgaria and Asia Minor. Not a lot is known about them and there is certainly controversy about their beliefs and practice. Much of what we know comes from hostile critics who labelled them as heretics. Some of their doctrines were certainly unbiblical. In contrast to the Paulicians, they adopted a rigidly ascetic life-style. They despised marriage, and condemned the eating of meat and drinking of wine.

The Bogomiles, however, rejected the superstitions associated with the sacraments and baptism and advocated simple piety. As one of their persecutors said:

> "They bid those who listen to their doctrines to keep the commandments of the gospel and to be meek and merciful and of brotherly love." (Euthymius).

Their custom was to meet together for a common meal. They were also probably the first door-to-door evangelists. It was said of them that "they got into private homes and made converts."

One of their most outstanding preachers was a doctor called Basil (1070-1119) who spent 40 years in tireless preaching. He was invited by the Emperor Alexius to Constantinople under the false pretext of wanting to hear his preaching. Basil was arrested and imprisoned for years before being burnt at the stake in 1119 as he refused to recant his doctrines. This kind of trickery would be tried centuries later on the likes of Jan Hus and Martin Luther.

In Bosnia, the Bogomiles had their greatest growth. Kulin Ban, the ruler of Bosnia, his family, the Roman Catholic Bishop of Bosnia and 10,000 Bosnians joined the Bogomile church in 1199. Miroslav, the Prince of Herzegovina, also joined the Bogomile Church. The country ceased to be Catholic and experienced a time of prosperity that has remained proverbial ever since. There were no priests. The churches were guided by a group of elders chosen by lot. Meetings could be held in any house and regular meeting places were plain without bells or altars. A part of the earnings of the brethren was set aside for the relief of sick believers and the poor and for the support of missionaries. During those few short years, apostolic Christianity was practised in Bosnia on a scale never seen before.

However, in 1203 under political threats from Pope Innocent III and the King of Hungary, the country reverted to a Catholic state-church. This action did not halt the spread of the Bogomiles into Croatia, Dalmatia, Istria and Slavonia. In the end the Pope ordered the King of Hungary to invade Bosnia and the country was devastated. An inquisition was set up in 1291 with Dominican and Franciscan priests competing to apply its terror techniques to exterminate these believers. How different the history of Bosnia and Yugoslavia might have been had the Bogomiles continued to have an influence.

9

THE MIDDLE AGES

(AD 1000-1500)

The 10th and 11th centuries were a period of degeneracy for the papacy. It had become the tool of violent Roman nobles and was a farce. In 1046 there were three men each claiming the title of Pope. The deeply religious Henry III, a German king and Holy Roman Emperor from 1039, was responsible for the cleansing of the papacy. He marched on Rome, summoned the Synod of Sutri, which deposed all three popes and installed a German, Clement II. The Roman nobles were forcibly subdued. Henry III appointed the next three popes, all Germans and all zealous for reform. During his life, both emperor and pope worked in amicable partnership. After his death, however, the papacy began to assert its independence and authority over the State.

Henry IV, another German king followed as Holy Roman Emperor in 1056. He needed the church's backing to contain the rising civil unrest in the Empire. Just as victory was won against Saxony in 1075, Pope Gregory VII (also known as Hildebrand) forbade lay investiture, thus denying Henry IV a voice in the selection of German church officials. He indignantly deposed Pope Gregory, to which the Pope responded by excommunicating Henry IV in 1076. This, as we have already seen, was the ultimate weapon of the Church. In 1077, Henry had to humiliate himself before Pope Gregory in Canossa, Italy. He received absolution but his royal powers were not reinstated. Many of the German princes and nobles supported Pope Gregory, and a new king, Rudolph of Swabia, was elected with Gregory's support. Civil war followed and Gregory excommunicated Henry again. This time, with popular opinion against the Pope, Henry IV again deposed Gregory and set up Clement III as his anti-pope and was crowned by Clement in 1084. These antics showed the world the mockery of the whole system. The Church was more interested in politics than in piety. As a part of the establishment, the Church was intricately enmeshed in the skulduggery of political intrigues. This was a far cry from the New Testament Church.

Henry's last years saw the collapse of the imperial government because of the revolts of his sons. Resulting from these wars was the growth of feudalism and princely sovereignty in Germany.

The struggle between Pope Gregory VII and Emperor Henry IV, Church and State, highlights several issues:

1) The civil governments had a century of power over church appointments, known as lay investiture. Gregory sought to reverse this so that the Church could have control over the State. He did not like being subordinate to the Emperor. For most of the time during the next 500 years, the Pope was in control, no longer the servant of the imperial power. As Successor to Peter, Gregory saw his responsibilities as governing the Church, whose officers included bishops as well as kings. The Pope wanted to control Western Europe and his political ambitions were realised.

2) The Church was prepared to appeal to the German princes in its struggle against Henry IV. Part of this appeal was to the nationalism of the princes who did not like Henry IV. The other part was of a wholly spiritual nature. By fighting for the Pope, the princes would be on God's side. This kind of approach would be repeated later, especially during the Reformation.

3) The Church was prepared to use force to establish its earthly kingdom. Gregory wished to lead a crusade to the Holy Land

which would lead to the unification of eastern and western Christianity. He died just before the First Crusade.

These are misguided views of the Church as an earthly empire, the City of God as taught by Augustine. If it was really an earthly kingdom, it would have legitimate rights to use force. But it is not an earthly kingdom and cannot be imposed by force using earthly powers. Gregory also established the symbol of the papacy, the crossed keys of St Peter, as the right to rule over State and Church.

The Crusades

The Crusades (Latin crux meaning "cross") were based on a powerful combination: misguided idealism and greed. Between 1095 and 1270, there were eight Crusades to the Holy Land, which was in Muslim hands. The first was led by a maniac, Peter the Hermit. It was launched with a massacre of thousands of Jews, particularly in German towns, in what was to become almost the traditional beginning to every expedition. Out of 600,000 men, only a bare 10 per cent arrived in Palestine. Most died in the high mountains of Turkey. The Crusaders took Jerusalem by violence on July 15, 1099. The city was pillaged and its women raped. Jews taking refuge in their synagogues were burnt alive. The Crusaders established the Church in Jerusalem.

The military orders of the Church were formed during this time. An occupying army needed castles to house the Crusaders. All the important Crusader fortresses belonged to the two great military orders - the Knights Templar and the Hospitallers. These orders were founded soon after the First Crusade captured Jerusalem, and their members swore the same vows as a monk - poverty, chastity, obedience - but their function was to fight. The Hospitallers soon became quite unashamedly military monks. These Crusaders were motivated by a misguided idealism. They viewed the Church as an earthly kingdom, a Christendom within which it was their God-given right and duty to use the sword to kill the infidels and recapture the Holy Land.

In addition to their misguided idealism, the Crusaders were also motivated by greed. People were offered all kinds of incentives to join the Crusades - absolution from sins, simony (buying of spiritual benefits), release from purgatory (the place of temporal punishment after death), debts cancelled and pardon from crimes. The list was a long one. It attracted all kinds of unsavoury characters who wanted to join in the rampage.

Richard of England and Philip of France were both caught up in the Crusades. One of the most tragic was the Children's Crusade. This saw 2,000 children marching to the Holy Land. The Pope claimed that angels would protect them and provide their food, yet not one survived the journey. The last Crusade was an utter failure. The entire army died of thirst while under siege. In 1270, Europe breathed a sigh of relief as the Pope called off the Crusades.

Despite this unmitigated disaster, the Church did not learn that God was not on its side fighting against the Muslims because he did not approve of the Church's actions. The Church was in a state of drunkenness because of its wealth and power. It felt invincible but was not. The Church had believed its own lie about its supremacy and infallibility. In refusing to listen to the truth, the Church opened itself up to self-deception on a grand scale. There was no soul-searching over this horrific failure. Unlike the nation of Israel when defeated by the army of Ai because of the sin of Achan (Josh. 7), this whole shameful episode was simply forgotten, buried in the deep recesses of the Church's subconscious. Not only was there no self-examination by the Church, there was no repentance either. This episode saw a brutality and savagery against Jews and Muslims of an unprecedented order. Christians owe it to them to repent for the diabolical deeds carried out against their forefathers in the name of Christ. It is a sign of grace and maturity that recent Catholic leaders have examined this episode with pain.

In England, there is an excellent youth organisation called Crusaders. My son is a member, and some leaders are friends and wonderful Christians. But I wonder at the insensitivity of the name Crusaders in the light of church history. What would we think of a Christian organisation called the Auschwitzers? Perhaps it is time for some reflection and change to demonstrate that we have learnt something from past failures.

The Inquisition

From using force outside the Church, the Pope turned to using force within. It was almost as if there were political and military aggression within the Church that needed some outlet. At the Council of Toulouse in 1229, the Inquisition was made a permanent institution. The Council also decreed that no parts of the Bible could be translated into the common language for the laity. Despite this decree there were many vernacular translations of the Bible in the late Middle Ages. Between 1231 and 1235, Pope Gregory IX was responsible for setting up the Inquisition to root out the heretics and dissenters on whom the military might of the State would be used.

The Dominicans and Franciscans were most often chosen as papal inquisitors. The Dominican order was founded in 1216 by a Spaniard, St Dominic, a contemporary of St Francis. Where Francis brought a much-needed simplicity to the Church, Dominic injected a new intellectual energy. Soon the most distinguished teachers at Oxford or Paris were Dominicans, or Black Friars as they were known because of their mode of dress. Dominic's first interest had been in preaching against "heresy". On his death, his wandering friars were a natural choice as inquisitors. The most notorious Grand Inquisitor of all, Torquemada of Spain, had ample opportunities to exercise his machinery of torture.

Spain had both Muslims and Europe's largest and most prosperous community of Jews. Granada was the last Spanish city to remain in Muslim hands. Using money they had seized from the Jews, King Ferdinand and Queen Isabella of Spain, with the dreaded Torquemada's approval, attacked the Muslims of Granada. The Muslims were offered the choice of burning the Koran and becoming baptised Christians, or leaving. Granada was finally captured. The Jews of Spain had already faced a similar choice earlier in 1492. In March, Ferdinand and Isabella took Torquemada's advice and signed a decree that all Jews must leave the country by the end of July. Almost 200,000 went, many going to Constantinople, a Muslim city which welcomed them. The country which had been the most tolerant in medieval Europe became notorious as the most intolerant of them all.

All manner of torture was used to secure profession of faith and recanting of heresy. Those deemed heretics who refused to recant were handed over to the civil authority for burning, because the Church did not officially participate in the shedding of blood. This was some neat justification on the part of the Church. It could claim that technically it did not participate in any murder, torture or violence.

Pope and politics

The 13th century closed with an unprecedented abdication of Pope Celestine V in 1294. This presented an interesting new problem for the Church: "Can the Pope, the Vicar of Christ, resign from his high office?" The authorities were left without an option. His successor was Pope Boniface VIII (1294-1303), whose reign was marked by conflicts between State and Church. In 1296 he passed a bull Clericis laicos limiting the power of kings to tax their clergy. France retaliated by prohibiting the export of bullion and England threatened to remove royal protection from the clergy. In the end, Boniface caved in to pressure from the French and abandoned Clericis laicos. This was not the end of the story. In 1301 a French bishop was arrested by the State for treason. The Pope demanded his release, which was refused. Boniface reactivated Clericis laicos and issued another bull, Ausculta fili, emphasising the pope's superiority over secular rulers.

In reply the French King, Philip IV stirred up public opinion against the Pope and sent Nogaret, his agent to bring back the Pope where his fate would be decided. Meanwhile, Boniface excommunicated the French king. Finally in September 1303, Nogaret with the help of the Italian Colonna family (great rivals of the Pope) attacked Boniface's forces at Anagni. With the aid of the townsfolk, Boniface escaped to Rome where he died a month later. These unseemly squabbles between Church and State, pope and politics, recurred again and again until the end of the Middle Ages. But is this what the Church is about? Is this the Church that Jesus intended?

The Avignon Papacy

These antics left the College of Cardinals, responsible for electing the Pope, divided into pro- and anti-French factions. As a result of French pressure, the Archbishop of Bordeaux was elected Pope in 1305, taking the name Clement V (1264-1314). He is best remembered as the Pope who moved the papacy from Rome to Avignon in southern France. For most of the 14th century, no Pope actually lived in Rome. There were protests about this "scandal". This "Avignon Captivity" remained for 70 years until Pope Urban V and his successor, Pope Gregory XI (1370-8), at last returned the papacy to Rome in 1367 and 1377. A number of significant changes took place during the reign of the Popes in Avignon. Clement V approved plans by the French king to destroy the Order of the Knights Templar, which had effectively become a huge banking corporation throughout Europe. While the official reason for this was that the Templars practised sodomy and idolatry, the real reason was to get at their wealth. In France, the greatest benefactor was the King himself. Clement V also introduced French bishops into the Italian-dominated College of Cardinals. Another notable Pope of this period was Pope John XXII (1316-34) who was one of the greatest of papal financiers. His interest was to create new ways of increasing papal income and influence through out Christendom.

Pope Clement VI (1291-1352) is remembered as a forerunner of the great Renaissance popes. He had a magnificent court, lavished money on pomp and ceremonies, and was accused of nepotism and immorality. In 1348, the city of Avignon was officially purchased by the papacy during his reign. There were calls for reform to end the waste of money. With the Pope away in Avignon, inter-family quarrels and battles grew out of control in Italy, especially in the papal states. To regain power over these states and to satisfy the growing demand for the return of the Pope to Rome, steps were taken to prepare for the return of the papacy. This was completed by Pope Gregory XI in 1377.

The papacy had at last returned to the Eternal City. All this while, the papacy was becoming more bureaucratic, centralised and expensive! The papal palace alone employed some 500 people. It is estimated that the average income for Pope John XXII was about a quarter of a million gold florins and that of Pope Gregory XI, half a million. With this growing institution, the Popes became more and more preoccupied with financial rather than spiritual matters. Papal favour and privileges were given in exchange for income. The growing costs of the papacy, its inner divisions and wars of the Italian princes for control were features of papal life towards the end of the 14th century.

The Papal Schism

Towards the end of this period, there was another struggle for papal power. Again two Popes fought for power. After the death of Pope Gregory XI, angry crowds gathered in Rome to demand the appointment of an Italian Pope. The cardinals eventually agreed and elected Urban VI (1378-89). He proved too autocratic for the cardinals, who elected a new man, Clement VII (d.1394) in his place. Armed battle for control of Rome resulted. Clement VII retreated to Avignon in 1381. Italy, Germany, Hungary and England supported Urban VI whilst France, Spain and Scotland supported Clement VII in Avignon. This was the beginning of the Great Schism, a split at the very top of church government which polarised Europe. Unlike earlier schisms, the division originated in the papal court itself among the College of Cardinals. Neither pope was willing to compromise. Urban VI even had some of his unbending cardinals tortured to death. There were two Popes and two rival Colleges of Cardinals - one in Rome and the other in Avignon. The Council at Pisa was called in 1409 to resolve this embarrassing conflict. Neither Pope's successors attended. The council deposed both Popes and elected in their place Alexander V (1409-10). Neither the Avignon nor the Roman Pope recognised this new choice, with the result that there were three Popes where there had previously been two! This problem was not finally resolved until the Council of Constance (1414-18). In 1415, John XXIII was forced to give up his claim to the papacy, Gregory

XII resigned, and only one pope, the Spanish Benedict XIII, was left.

The State of the Church

Not only had the papacy degenerated, so had the church. During this period of unrest and divisions, many changes took place causing further distortions to the Church. Its evangelical roots were lost. Instead of Christ as its sole basis of faith, now there were confessions to priests and prayers to Mary and the saints. To these were added the worship of religious relics, idols, pilgrimages and superstitions of all sorts in order to be assured of salvation. Sacerdotalism was firmly entrenched by this stage, with salvation obtained through the sacraments.

The doctrine of transubstantiation, although in existence by the fourth century was finally defined and adopted by the Council of Trent (1545-63). This doctrine taught that Christ was present in the Eucharist in a literal manner and that he is offered up as a sacrifice at the altar. This was why no accidental dropping and spilling of bread or wine was allowed. In the Early Church, Clement of Alexandria (d.215) and Origen (d.253) saw the elements (the bread and wine) as symbols and taught that the presence of Christ at the Eucharist was spiritual. The idea of sacrifice and priesthood can, however, be detected by the time of Cyprian (d.258). Up until the third century however, these writers referred to a sacrifice of thanksgiving and an offering of the elements. It was not until the fourth century, with Cyril of Jerusalem and the compiler of the *Apostolic Constitution,* that we see the beginnings of the doctrine of transubstantiation.

The Eucharist then passed from a sacrifice of thanksgiving to a sacrifice of atonement, and from the offering of the elements to an offering of Christ. In place of the spiritual presence of Christ, it was believed that the elements became the "literal" body and blood of Christ either at the invocation of the Holy Spirit or through the words of the institution used at the Eucharist. The concept of the real presence of Christ in the elements and the identification with the sacrifice on the cross paved the way for the development of the Mass in the Middle Ages. Radbertus, a Benedictine monk, is credited with defining the doctrine of transubstantiation in 831. This was the position of the Church from the fourth century onwards, though it was not officially adopted until the Council of Trent more than 1,000 years later.

The doctrine of purgatory was clearly taught as biblical truth by fourth century Latin Fathers such as Augustine of Hippo. In Christendom, everyone believed that if they died forgiven and blessed by a priest, they were bound for heaven. They had no fear of hell but they did fear purgatory's pain. This was a temporal place of punishment between heaven and hell, for those whose sins have not been absolved in life. It is not hell because all those in purgatory are on their way to heaven. It is where everyone has to be cleansed of every sin committed during their lifetime before they can go on to heaven. In a sacral Christendom where everyone was a "Christian", there was no need to teach the doctrine of hell. When this was neglected, a new "threat" had to take its place to instil an element of fear into the people. Without some kind of a "stick" it would be difficult to govern the Church. Purgatory suited this purpose well. During the medieval period, this doctrine was popularised by Pope Gregory the Great (540-604), and further elaborations developed by Thomas Aquinas (1224-74). For instance, it was taught that the smallest pain in purgatory was worse than the greatest pain on earth. The souls could escape purgatory through the prayers and Masses offered for them by the Church.

The doctrines of indulgences and purgatory are bedfellows. Indulgences are the remissions of sins that are punishable in purgatory. The authority for granting indulgences rests with the Pope and his designated agents. Forms of indulgences include reciting certain prayers, performing certain works on special days, pilgrimages, reciting certain holy names at the hour of death and purchases of religious relics such as crucifixes, statues, medals and rosaries. The granting of indulgences really took off in the 11th century. During this time, indulgences were granted in return for relaxation of penance on condition that money was paid to the church or monastery. These was the beginnings of the "holy trade" as it became known. During the First Crusade in 1095, Pope Urban II granted remission of all penance to all who volunteered for the Crusade. Later this was extended to all those who made financial contributions to the Crusades. The Church very quickly saw this as an easy means of fund-raising. So it was that throughout the medieval period, clergymen and banker's agents could be seen everywhere collecting money in return for absolving the purchasers' sins. This was a hugely lucrative trade in which the Church had the monopoly. It was a scandal which was to eventually touch off the Reformation.

Evangelical, pentecostal and radical elements were lost to the church at this stage. Only the institutional and sacramental aspects were retained, though with distortions. The Church was more a political and business corporation than a community of believers. It had a huge and expensive bureaucracy to maintain. Its sacramental aspects had become more and more superstitious and elaborate. How the mighty had fallen. The Church to whom Christ said he would return, was anything but spotless and without blemish. How God must have been grieved by all this.

The church had began to think of itself as Christ and the Pope as the Vicar of Christ on earth. Everyone had to come to it for confession and sacrament. There was a tragic confusion between the divine and infallible Head which is Christ, and the human and fallible Body which is the Church. Throughout the Middle Ages, when the Pope spoke, it was taken as if Christ had spoken.

In 1453, the Turks captured the second most important religious centre of power in Christendom next to Rome - Constantinople. Unlike the fall of Rome in the fifth century, there was no gnashing of teeth. The patriarch of Constantinople continued to keep his office in the city and the Turks treated the Christians with generosity. In fact, the Greek Orthodox Church survived four centuries of Ottoman Turkish rule. In contrast with the Crusades and the Inquisitions, Christians should understandably hang their heads in shame at such treatment. Muslims have been more honourable in their treatment of Christians.

10

PROTEST MOVEMENTS

AD 1000-1500

This was another dark period in the history of the Church which saw the rise of a significant number of protest movements around Europe. They gathered such momentum that it ultimately led to the Reformation. Like brooks they merged and formed streams until they became a great river whose waters broke through the barriers of the establishment. In the midst of the darkness of this period, these movements shone as light. Where sin abounded, it seems that grace abounded even more.

Albigenses

The main centre of the Albigensian churches was the town of Albi in the Provence region of southern France. One of the rulers of this area, Count Raymond VI of Toulouse, was a leading supporter and under his protection the churches flourished. In many respects they were Catholic churches with an emphasis on radical discipleship and personal piety.

The doctrines of the Albigenses have been the subject of some controversy. Some who were mystics and followers of Manichaeism were falsely accused of being connected to them. This supposed association with some of the followers of Mani was used to tarnish the reputation of the Albigenses. There is evidence that they were fairly unorthodox in their beliefs and behaviour. They opposed marriage, procreation and the use of material things in worship. However, there is also evidence at a trial by the authorities that their doctrines did not differ significantly from the Catholics. They were only condemned because they refused the oath of allegiance to the State and believed all human government to be evil. In lifestyle, their simplicity and piety were in contrast to the self-indulgence of the clergy. Some of them gave themselves to travelling and preaching and were called "the Perfect". Taking Matthew 19:21 literally, they possessed nothing and had no home. In 1201, during a visit of a preacher from Albania, revival was started in the South of France.

The growth of the Albigensian churches worried the Pope. In 1209, Pope Innocent III proclaimed a crusade against the Albigenses. Indulgences were sold to hundreds of thousands of people to persuade them to join in the crusade under the leadership of Simon de Monfort, an ambitious, ruthless and cruel military leader. When the town of Beziers was taken, not one out of the tens of thousands was taken alive. In La Minerve, when 140 believers were caught in prayer, De Monfort told them to be converted to the Catholic faith or be burnt. They answered that they owned no papal or priestly authority, only that of Christ and his Word. The fire was lit and all 140 entered the flames. The Inquisition was established near this spot in 1210 under the superintendence of Dominic. The Inquisition finished what the crusade had left undone. Many Albigenses fled to the Balkan countries. The civilisation of Provence disappeared and the independent provinces of the south were incorporated into the kingdom of France.

Francis of Assisi

St Francis represents the protest movement within the Roman Catholic church at this time. Whilst others had formed protest movements outside the Catholic Church, he sought to stay within the official Church to bring about reforms. In 1209, at the start of the repression of the Albigenses, Francis, aged 25, heard the command of Jesus to go out and preach (Matt 10) during the Mass one day. He felt himself called to preach in poverty and humility. From this rapidly sprang the order of Franciscan Friars or Grey Friars. They tried to restore simplicity to the Church but failed as it was too set in its ways, not wanting to give up the trappings of wealth and influence it enjoyed. The Franciscans in the end became pious beggars.

Francis was a wonderful preacher, drawing large crowds with his sincerity, devotion and joyous nature. He was the first missionary to the Muslims when he visited the Sultan on his own and in humility, not with 600,000 soldiers. After his death in 1226, the order was divided into the stricter friars, "Spirituali," and the more lax ones. The strict group, with their vows of poverty, were persecuted and four were burnt in Marseilles in 1318. That same year, the Pope made the historic declaration that the teaching that Christ and his apostles possessed nothing was a heresy. The Franciscans were obviously a thorn in the flesh of the establishment. Through their radical life of obedience to the gospel, they spoke out against the corruption in the Church and its immense wealth. They were disturbing the conscience of the Church and therefore had to be silenced. It was the first time that the Pope had sanctioned the murder of members of a Catholic monastic order. It seems that once the killing started with Priscillian in 385, there was no end to violence in the name of God. The Franciscans, together with the Dominicans, were later to be involved in perpetrating and executing the Inquisitions.

Other Radical Catholics

Besides St Francis, there were other reformers within the Catholic Church at this time. Arnold of Brescia was a member of the Augustinian order. He advocated the necessity of apostolic poverty in the Church, repudiated the power of the hierarchy and argued that the sacraments were invalid when administered by clergy with worldly possessions. He was excommunicated for his views, condemned as a heretic, hanged and burnt in 1155.

Pierre de Brueys taught against the superstition of venerating crucifixes and the doctrine of transubstantiation, and insisted that no one should be baptised until fully able to reason. He was joined by Henry of Cluny, whose convincing expositions of Scripture and his zeal turned many to repentance and faith. He was ultimately opposed by Bernard of Clairvaux, who was at that time the most influential and powerful man in Europe. Henry was arrested by the clergy, imprisoned and probably put to death in 1147.

Bernard of Clairvaux, the son of a French baron, withdrew with 12 friends to form a Cistercian community in Clairvaux, France. He was described as rigidly orthodox, aggressively self-righteous, deeply pious and ascetic. Through force of personality he became the most powerful man of his time, even to choosing Eugenius III as the Pope. In public he backed the papacy and was a formidable opponent of heretics and dissenters. He was a vigorous advocate of the Crusades and of Holy War theology. It has been said that he set back the Reformation by at least two centuries. In private however, Bernard had a deep devotion and love for his Lord. He is probably best remembered for his hymns such as "O sacred head once wounded", "Jesus Thou joy of loving hearts" and "Jesus the very thought of Thee". Two great admirers of his in later years were Luther and Calvin.

These were the voices of dissent within the Catholic Church. Things were stirring at a time when the Church was carrying out damage limitation exercises on many fronts. The fabric of the Church was being shaken. Doubts were being planted in the minds of those prepared to think and study the Bible. Questions relating to creed and conduct were being provoked by these Catholic reformers.

Waldensians

For centuries, in the Alpine valleys of Vallenses, France, congregations of believers widely known as Waldensians had existed. They claimed their origins went back to apostolic times. They were also called "Friends of God" by some. They faithfully maintained the truth in both their creed and conduct. Their doctrines included:

1) An evangelical obedience to the gospel, especially the Sermon on the Mount. They laid great emphasis on the value of practical piety. Following Christ by imitating His example was their chief aim.

2) A "Donatist" aversion to recognising the ministry of unworthy living priests.

3) A belief in the work of the Spirit, visions and prophecies.

4) An emphasis on social renewal. They valued education as well as spirituality and developed an excellent schooling system.

5) A belief in apostolic succession through the laying on of hands. They claimed that the apostolic succession had been passed on to the Waldensian Church in this way.

6) The Waldensian apostles had no property or goods or home or family. Their life was one of self-denial, without money, without a second suit; their needs were met by the believers among whom they ministered the Word in pairs.

Radical Waldensians today prefer to derive their name from one of their most able leaders, Peter Waldo (or Valdes). They also recognise their debt to the radical reformers within the Catholic Church of the time such as Arnold of Brescia, Pierre de Bruey and Henry of Cluny.

Peter Waldo (1160-217) was a successful merchant and banker. In obedience to the call of God on his life, he sold his properties, provided for his family, gave the rest to the poor and started studying the Scriptures and preaching. His followers, called "The Poor Men of Lyon", gave a tremendous impetus to missionary activities across Europe. Waldo himself continued his travels until he reached Bohemia where he died in 1217 after laying the foundations for the coming spiritual revival in that country during the time of Jan Hus. It was said that during the "First"(Hussite) Reformation, Waldensian influence was all over Europe. We are undoubtedly indebted to them for their faithfulness in preserving the biblical testimony which was to be used by God to contribute to the Reformation. This was a stream that had flowed strongly, carrying many of the New Testament truths lost in the official Church.

For a century, from 1380, the Waldensians were persecuted by Pope Clement VII and Innocent VIII. During these harsh times, many thousands were killed and there were mass migrations of the Waldensians across Europe in search of religious toleration. Waldensian churches remain to this day in Italy. There are some 20,000 members, but it has missions in Africa and South America. They have schools, homes for the aged, orphanages, hospitals and a publishing house.

The Waldensians were like springs in the desert. God had raised these groups up in the heart of Europe, in France. We now turn to what God was raising up in the western corner of Europe, in England.

Wycliffe and the Lollards

John Wycliffe (1329-84) was a Yorkshireman and the most eminent scholar in Oxford of his day. He was known as "Doctor Evangelicus" and protested against the numerous papal abuses. His courage and outspokenness earned him the wrath of the Pope. He had the rare honour of having five decrees or bulls against him from the Pope. But such was his standing as a scholar and a Christian that he, under the royal protection of John of Gaunt, was never arrested and never responded to the summons to appear in Rome to give an account of his teachings against the Church.

Wycliffe saw much that was wrong with the Church. His teachings included the following themes:

1) He attacked the corrupt practices of the Catholic Church.

2) He believed that "the gospel of Jesus Christ is the only source of true religion". Scripture is the sole authority.

3) He taught that each person was directly responsible to God. There was no need for intermediaries - priests or Pope. He taught the priesthood of all believers.

4) He repudiated transubstantiation and attacked the magical elements of the sacrament.

5) He attacked the institution of the papacy and challenged its legitimacy.

6) He repudiated indulgences and the underlying corrupt practices of fund-raising.

7) He wanted to abolish all religious orders, believing that discipleship should be lived out in the world. The religious orders had become powerful and wealthy institutions riddled with corruption.

In addition to teaching, Wycliffe was also a prolific writer. His major work was *Summa Theologica*. He and his associates also found time to translate the Latin Vulgate Bible into English, leaving a lasting legacy to the Church. Wycliffe understood that there had to be a return to the Bible if change were to come about in the Church. He realised that Christians had to have access to the Bible. "I am going to cause the plough boys to know the Book" summed up his vision and commitment.

Here then was a brilliant scholar, who through his studies used Scriptures to expose the errors of the Church. But here too was an apostle, a prophet who understood that his learning needed to move beyond the ivory towers of Oxford University into the fields. He gave himself to both tasks with equal effectiveness.

Wycliffe died of a stroke at his home in Lutterworth in 1384. The fact that someone as prominent and outspoken as Wycliffe was allowed a peaceful death, one not usually granted to radicals, is a testimony to the respect he commanded even among those who hated his teaching.

Among students at Oxford who were influenced was Jerome of Prague who carried Wycliffe's teachings back to his city. This teaching was passed on to Jan Hus, theological doctor and preacher in Prague and Confessor to the Queen of Bohemia. Hus and his followers adopted the teachings of Wycliffe and kept them alive until the Reformation era. No wonder Wycliffe has been called the "Morning Star of the Reformation". More than any one else before him, Wycliffe articulated the major issues regarding the Church and laid the biblical groundwork for the Reformation. During Wycliffe's time, a movement grew up based upon his radical teachings even though Wycliffe was not its leader.

These were the Lollards or "babblers" or "lullabyes", so called because they sang or rhymed the gospel throughout the villages of England. They were originally composed of Oxford scholars led by Nicholas of Hereford, the translator of the first Lollard Bible. From Oxford, the movement spread until it was estimated that 50 per cent of the population in certain parts of the country were converted. It was said that two men could not be found together without one being a Lollard or a Wycliffite. This was a very powerful movement of the Spirit. Among its leaders were John Purvey, Wycliffe's secretary, and Sir John Oldcastle, a distinguished soldier who escaped capture on many occasions but was finally caught and hanged. He was the first English nobleman to die for his faith. John Ball was also a leading figure among the peasants preaching to thousands in the open fields. The Peasant's Revolt (1377-81) was crushed and iniquitous laws passed to keep down the labourers.

Despite attempts to persecute and crush the movement, by 1395 the Lollards had become an organised sect with specially ordained ministers. They even had spokesmen in Parliament and a large following among the noble and artisan classes. Their beliefs are summarised in the "Twelve Conclusions" which expressed disapproval of the hierarchy in the Church, transubstantiation, clerical celibacy, the Church's temporal power, prayers for the dead, pilgrimages, images, war and art in the Church. The Reformation spirit was really fermenting in England during this time.

Jan Hus and the Hussites

The Reformation spirit was passed from England across the Continent into Bohemia (part of the modern Czech Republic). In the economy of God, the two ends of Europe would be engulfed in the flames of the Reformation.

Jan Hus heard the radical teachings of Wycliffe from Jerome of Prague in 1401 when he was the Rector and preacher of the Bethlehem Chapel, the centre of Czech preaching after the tradition of previous Czech reform movements. For Hus, the teachings of Wycliffe echoed his own searchings, and from the moment he heard them he was committed to reforming the Church. However, not everyone received Wycliffe's teaching with favour. In 1403, Johann Hubner, a master at Prague University, selected 45 theses from Wycliffe's writing and secured their condemnation by the Pope. This divided the University which had had a long history of rivalry between the German academics, who supported the Pope, and the Czech academics, who supported the reforms of Wycliffe. The Pope, through the Archbishop of Prague, excommunicated Hus and had Wycliffe's writings publicly burnt. But the King of Bohemia, Wenceslas, with the nobility, the University authorities and the majority of the people, supported Hus and his teaching. The German faction at the university was ousted and Hus became the rector of the new Czech University.

This was an exciting time of learning the truth from the Bible, a "springtime in Prague". There was a freedom of conscience never felt before. There was an openness to question traditions. There was a real buzz about the place and students packed lecture halls because of their hunger for God's Word. The people felt the hand of God in their situation as if they were on the verge of something momentous. The extent of the reforms during the time of Hus and later the Unitas Fratrum has led some to call this the "First Reformation".

The atmosphere of Prague can best be seen by Hus' conflicts with Pope John XXIII over the sale of indulgences to finance his crusade against King Ladislas of Naples. Hus vehemently denounced this "trafficking in sacred things" as a heresy. His preaching ignited the Prague populace, who rose in revolt and burnt a copy of a papal bull. Hus was declared under major excommunication by the Pope.

The Catholic hierarchy had a time bomb on their hands with

Hus. In 1414, the Council of Constance was called to resolve two issues. One was to decide who should be Pope. There were three contenders for the position at the time. All three were dethroned and a new Pope, Martin V, chosen in their place. The second issue was to decide on a strategy to combat the teachings of Wycliffe and Hus. Obviously the Catholic authorities were concerned about the signs of stirrings right across Europe because these teachings had struck a chord in many hearts. Furthermore, they struck at the very core of the Catholic Church. These teachings were dangerously close to the bone. Left unchecked, there could be rebellion right across Christendom and it would topple the very structure of the institution of which they were guardians.

The Holy Roman Emperor, Sigismund, promised Hus safe conduct to explain his teachings. In spite of this imperial promise, Hus was captured, imprisoned, tortured to make him recant and later burnt at the stake. It was a cynical betrayal by the authorities. If they thought that by silencing Hus in this way, they could remove the threats to their house of cards, they were wrong. Hus' teachings lived on in Prague among his followers. The flame that had been ignited by Wycliffe and fanned into a fire by Hus could not be put out. Truth cannot be suppressed forever. The day of the revealing of God's truth was dawning.

When Hus was condemned to death, the Church authorities exhumed the bones of Wycliffe and burnt them. This took place 44 years after his death. This indicates who the Church authorities regarded as being the instigator of these heresies. Such then was the condemnation heaped upon Wycliffe because of the troubles he had caused that, even though dead and buried, the authorities had no compunction about burning his bones as a public declaration that he was regarded as a heretic. They threw his ashes into the River Swift in Lutterworth. It was said then: "as the River Swift will bear the ashes into the River Avon, which will flow into the River Severn and into the [Bristol] channel before getting to the ocean, so will the teachings of John Wycliffe spread through all the world". This was indeed prophetic.

Unitas Fratrum

The spirit of reform was maintained after Hus' death by Jakoubek, a colleague of Hus and Peter Chelcicky (d.1460) who wrote *Net of Faith* in 1440. The preaching continued despite the political threats.

In 1457 a congregation of the brethren in Prague under Gregory (known as the Patriarch), moved to the village of Kunwald, where they founded a community. Many joined them there. Some were followers of Peter Chelcicky, some from the Waldensian churches and some students from Prague. They returned to early church practices with community of goods and believers' baptism as was the custom among the Waldensian churches, and were governed by pastors and elders. They formally declared their separation from the Church of Rome and called themselves Unitas Fratrum, the United Brethren. They were also known as the Bohemian Brethren or Moravian Brethren. Here were the first-fruits of the reformation teachings of Wycliffe and Hus.

These believers caught the New Testament vision for the church and with courage sought to live out their faith. While they did not believe in ordination, nevertheless one of their leaders, Matthias of Kunwald, was sent to be ordained by the Waldensian Bishop Stephen in Austria, thus marking their continued connection with the Waldensian brethren.

Despite much persecution, their numbers and influence increased throughout Bohemia. Changes took place as people of education, position and wealth became members and leadership passed out of the hands of simpler brethren to those learned men. Lukas of Prague (d.1528) was one of the most prominent. In 1547, King Ferdinand mobilised an army to crush the Brethren. Many escaped to Poland, where they joined the cause of reform and eventually merged with the Calvinist Church. In Bohemia, the leader John Augusta was tortured and imprisoned for 16 years.

Between 1609 and 1620, the Brethren returned to their homeland. Then the Battle of White Mountain (1620) took place.

Catholic forces virtually destroyed Protestantism in Bohemia and Moravia for more than 150 years. Scattered groups of survivors later accepted the invitation of Count Zinzendorf to join the Moravian community called "Herrnhut" in 1721.

The Unitas Fratrum was therefore influenced by two major streams. There were the radical teachings of Wycliffe and Hus on the one hand, and the radical lifestyle of the Waldensians on the other. Both were combined in this movement. Survivors of this movement then carried these truths with them when they joined the Moravian Church of Count Zinzendorf. And so the flame was being passed on, the historical and spiritual continuity of these movements was established.

Brethren of the Common Life

At one end of Europe, the teachings of Wycliffe had set England on fire. At the other end of Europe the fiery preaching of Hus had also started to rage. God would now cause the centre and heart of Europe to spark into flames too. Closely connected with the Unitas Fratrum was a movement called the Brethren of the Common Life, who established a network of schools throughout the Netherlands and northwest Germany in the 14th and 15th century. These schools were founded by Gerhard Groote who started the first in Deventer, Holland. The key principle behind their teaching was that "the root of study and the mirror of life must in the first instance be the gospel of Christ". These schools had as many as 2,000 pupils.

Among the leading pupils was Thomas á Kempis (1380-1471) who wrote a manual of devotion, *The Imitation of Christ* to help the soul achieve communion with Christ. This became a classic in its day. It calls the Christian into a life of radical discipleship and reflects the teachings of this movement. Through scholarship of the Gospels and meditation on Christ, this movement showed up the true Christ and the required standard of a Christian life. At the same time it also exposed the low level of spirituality in the official Church. *The Imitation of Christ* was an important contribution as the Church headed towards the Reformation.

The most illustrious pupil of this movement however was Erasmus (1466-1536). He became the leading Christian humanist of his day, wishing to reform the Church through scholarship and instruction in the teachings of Christ. During a brief visit to England, Erasmus met John Colet, who encouraged him to apply his humanistic interests to biblical scholarship. Erasmus, in his critical studies of the Greek texts, took another step towards the Reformation. He was a prolific writer, and his Greek New Testament contributed significantly to the Reformation. It has been said that "Erasmus laid the egg that Luther hatched". Erasmus together with Johann von Staupitz, Bible professor at Wittenberg University, was to have a profound influence on Martin Luther.

Friends of God

In the 14th and 15th century, there was a growth in interest in mysticism as a reaction against the worldliness of the Church. A group of these mystics of Germany became known as Friends of God or *Gottesfreunde*. They stayed within the confines of the Catholic Church but sought through their preaching and writing to call it back to a deeper level of spirituality. They were conscious of the spiritual bankruptcy of the Church and its authorities and believed that the way back to God was through piety and meditative contemplation.

One of the early German mystics was Eckhart von Hochheim (c.1260 - 1327), better known as Meister Eckhart. He was a noted preacher, though many of his sermons were delivered to nuns in convents. In 1326 he was accused of heresy but appealed to Rome. His ethical teachings were of such a high standard that it was difficult to convict him. His followers included Henry of Suso (c.1300-66) and Johann Tauler (c.1300-61).

It has been said that Eckhart "bridged scholasticism and mysticism, but Tauler translated the academic approach to spirituality into a practical Christianity of high personal demands, designed for all men". Tauler saw that spirituality was not only for the elite but for everyone. He also saw the poverty of the Church in lacking experience of God. Amid all the trappings of religion there was no sense of the presence of God and there was an acute absence of a knowledge of the holy.

Tauler owed a great debt to the Waldensian layman, Nicholas of Basle, who advised him to stop preaching and meditate, which he did for two years with remarkable results. Luther read Tauler with enthusiasm and acknowledged his influence on his devotion to Christ.

11

THE REFORMATION

The stage was set. Right across Europe pockets of spiritual fires were burning away. Events were building up to an explosion because people were reading the Bible and discovering the truth for themselves. The abuses of the papacy and the Church could not continue, for they were leading to gross economic and social injustices and questions were being asked which could no longer be suppressed.

There was also the contribution of the Renaissance, an age of discovery in both the material and intellectual realms. In the material, there was Columbus and the discovery of America; Copernicus and Galileo with discoveries in astronomy. It was the age of scientific enquiry. In the intellectual, it was the re-discovery of Greek culture, art and literature. With the fall of Constantinople, some Greek scholarship moved into Western Europe. Erasmus carried out his studies on the Greek New Testament and Hebrew Old Testament and produced an accurate edition of the Greek New Testament which would fuel the Reformation. The printing press was invented during this time, aiding the dissemination of Erasmus' work. But during this period of discovery, people saw that if man was intellectually better, he was not morally better. The Renaissance was intellectual advancement whereas the Reformation was moral improvement.

These were undoubtedly important factors leading up to the

Reformation. There is another factor. The Reformation saw the drawing together of several streams from across Europe - the Waldensians in France, Wycliffe in England, Hus in Prague, Erasmus and Tauler in Germany. These streams were converging to form a mighty river with some strong currents. Either the flood gates had to be opened or the river would burst through the barriers anyway. There was an inevitability about it all. God was on the move and he was unstoppable. It was a case of either swimming with the tide or being drowned.

Germany
Martin Luther (1483-1546)

Martin Luther was a German Augustinian monk and theologian who wrestled over his salvation. Despite his theological training and his monastic vows, he was deeply disturbed about the absence of assurance of his own salvation. The Church's doctrines of salvation by works and through the sacraments were unsatisfactory. When, therefore, an opportunity arose for him to visit Rome in 1510, Luther grabbed it and set out with high expectations of finding answers to his restless searching. He was going to be bitterly disappointed.

Expecting to be able to unburden his soul in confession and to seek pastoral counsel in Rome, Luther was shocked to find the priests there to be immoral, ignorant and miserable. He dutifully performed his pilgrimages to the seven main churches of the city, fasting all the way but horrified by the sight of people performing their human functions in the streets without any privacy. He crawled on his knees up the twenty-eight steps of the Scala Sancta, "moved" from Jerusalem, the staircase Christ was supposed to have ascended to Pilate, saying a Pater Noster on each step and for good measure kissing each piously in the hope of delivering a soul from purgatory. At the top of the stairs, Luther asked himself the question "How do I know this is true?" This was a deeply disconcerting doubt. Luther's son Paul claimed that his father told him that it was while he was ascending these steps that the text from Habakkuk came to him, "The righteous shall live by his faith", the text that led him finally to real faith. Every step Luther took was punctuated by disturbing doubts. He was dismayed to learn that the red-light district of Rome was frequented by the clergy and that Pope Alexander VI had mistresses and illegitimate children. He was distressed by the frivolity of the priests and the scandalous conduct of the cardinals. For Luther, the immorality of the priests and the lechery of the Pope could be forgiven as long as the Church had valid means of grace for salvation.

> "But if crawling up the very steps that Jesus climbed and repeating all the prescribed prayers would be of no avail, then another of the great grounds of hope had proved to be illusory" (Bainton).

Luther returned to Erfurt and was transferred to Wittenberg where he came under the guidance of Johann von Staupitz, the vicar of the Augustinian order. Miserable as he was, he continued to strive for peace in himself. He tried the way of good works and found he could not do enough to save himself. He tried appealing to the saints - he selected 21 of them as his special patrons, three for each day of the week but to no avail. He confessed frequently, often daily, and for as long as six hours on one occasion. Nothing gave him peace. Staupitz seeing this troubled man, suggested that he should study for a doctorate and take up the chair of Bible at the local university. Staupitz was wise enough to know that Luther would benefit from studying the Bible. We may be amazed that Luther himself had not thought to study the Bible in search of answers to his doubts. It was not that the Bible was inaccessible to Luther, but rather that he was following a prescribed course of theological training and the Bible, incredibly, was not a part of the syllabus!

Luther set himself to learn and expound the Scriptures. He started on the Psalms in 1513, Romans in 1515 and Galatians in 1516-17. These studies proved to be Luther's Damascus Road. There in his study in the monastery tower, Luther had his evangelical experience (later called his "Tower Experience") where he came to a full realisation of the meaning of justification by grace and through faith alone. The joy of his conversion showed up the emptiness and the errors of the Church, and Luther was now ready to become an instrument for change.

The opportunity arose during the occasion of the selling of indulgences for the building of a grandiose Basilica of St Peter in Rome. The Pope was Leo X, renowned for his ability to squander the resources of the Holy See on parties, gambling, sports and carousing. It was claimed that the resources of three papacies were dissipated by his profligacy. Pope Leo X had a building programme for a new Basilica of St Peter sufficiently splendid to house the bones of the apostles Peter and Paul. He needed money for this scheme. Albert of Brandenburg wanted to become the Primate of Germany and negotiated a suitably large sum of money with the Pope for his office. These negotiations were conducted through a German merchant bank called Fugger, which had a monopoly on papal finances in Germany. Albert had to pay the money to the Pope before he could be appointed to his new office. For this he had to borrow from the Fugger Bank, which then supervised the sale of the indulgences issued by the Pope. It was agreed that after expenses to Fuggers, half of the money would go to Rome and half to Albert. The more money collected, the more profit for Albert. To make matters worse, the proclamation of this indulgence was entrusted to a Dominican friar, Tetzel, an unsavoury character who was totally shameless in his promotion of the sale. It had all the trappings of an ecclesiastical circus.

This was too much for Luther. On October 31, 1517, Luther nailed the famous Ninety-five Theses to the door of Castle Church, Wittenberg. This was the traditional notice board to invite scholars and dignitaries to a public debate. Although the *Theses* were Luther's protest against the scandal of the indulgence traffic, they also attacked the practices and beliefs of the Pope and the Catholic Church. Unbeknown to Luther, the *Theses* were surreptitiously translated into German and printed. Within a very short time, Luther's Theses became the talk of Germany. Luther was a rather unsuspecting reformer - he really had not expected to cause such a stir. "He was like a man climbing a winding staircase of a church in the dark. In the blackness, he reached out to steady himself and his hand laid hold of a rope. He was startled to hear the clanging of a bell. This was the bell that sounded the first rounds of the Protestant Reformation." (Bainton)

Even more significant than this was his action on June 15, 1520, when Luther had a bonfire and burnt a number of documents. Among them:

1) A parchment with the Pope's signature excommunicating Luther from the Catholic Church;

2) A copy of the Canon Law by which he was supposed to live as a monk and priest;

3) Documents which Luther knew to be forgeries claiming that the Pope was the Vicar of Christ.

In burning these documents, Luther was effectively "burning his boat" in relation to the Catholic Church. This was a full-scale declaration of war against the papal authorities. Between 1517 and 1520, Luther had come to ask the questions that would strike at the very heart of the Catholic system. He started out by attacking the abuses of the system, the priests, sale of indulgences. It was intended as a spring-cleaning operation. But by 1520, he was attacking the very basis of the system, seeking to demolish it. These three years represent a time of deep thinking by Luther and he emerged with the basis of the Protestant Reformation. Luther championed the following truths:

a) Sola scriptura (Scripture only)

Luther was 20 years old before he read his first Bible. Above all else, Luther restored the authority of Scripture as the final arbiter of creed and conduct to the Church. He placed Scripture before traditions, truth before unity - though not always consistently, as we shall see.

b) Sola fide (Faith only)

The manifesto of the Reformation was "the just shall live by faith".

Luther had rediscovered the evangelical doctrine of salvation. We cannot buy or earn our salvation. We cannot be saved by the church or its sacraments without faith. It is only through faith in the Lord Jesus. Faith comes before works. Sadly however, teaching on justification was often not accompanied by that on sanctification.

c) Sola gratia (Grace only)

There is no grace in the sacraments that can save us. The grace of God is extended to us only in the person of Jesus and can only be received through Him.

d) Priesthood of Believers

Luther also attacked the very basis of the papacy. He challenged the notion that the Church and the Pope could do for the people what only Christ could do for them, saying: "I will have no priest but Christ, no vicar but the Holy Spirit." Luther was born into a pyramid hierarchy of pope, bishops, priests and laity. He modified this and talked in "theory" about the priesthood of all believers. In practice however, he retained the system of the clergy.

e) Sacraments

He reduced the number of sacraments from seven to three - baptism, the Lord's Supper and penance. This was later reduced to two. Luther also taught against the sale of indulgences and purgatory.

Luther's famous saying in defence of the faith at the Diet (Assembly) of Worms is worth quoting: "I cannot and I will not recant anything, for to go against conscience is neither right nor safe. Here I stand, I cannot do otherwise. God help me. Amen." His conscience was captive to the Word of God and would not allow him to accept the authority of the Church where it conflicted with the Scriptures.

In 1520 Luther published some of his most important reformation writings. In the Sermon on the Mass, he said that every Christian was a priest, so teaching the priesthood of all believers. On the papacy at Rome he branded the Pope as the real anti-Christ of whom the Scripture speaks. In The Address to the German Nobility, he denied the authority of the Pope over the civil rulers, denied that the Pope was the final interpreter of Scripture, decried the corruption of the Curia, the papal court and affirmed again the priesthood of all believers. In Concerning the Babylonian Captivity of the Church, he reduced the number of sacraments from seven to two.

In 1521, Luther stood before the Emperor in the Diet of Worms refusing to recant his doctrines unless convinced by Scripture. He was condemned by the Edict of Worms and declared an outlaw, and was taken to Wartburg Castle by order of Frederick the Wise, elector of Saxony for his own protection. It was here that he translated the New Testament from Greek to German.

Although an "outlaw" by this time, he was allowed to emerge briefly from hiding to Wittenberg in March 1522 to cope with the Wittenberg Movement. He found his followers advocating changes that went too far too quickly. In his absence, Karlstadt became the leading Reformer of Wittenberg supported by Melanchthon. On Christmas Day 1521, Karlstadt conducted the Mass in a new evangelical manner. The church was packed with 2,000 people and the communion was led by him without the usual vestments. It was conducted in an abbreviated Latin form of the Mass from which all references to sacrifice had been removed. When the bread and the wine were offered to the people, Karlstadt began to speak in German. This was an earth-shattering experience for all.

Luther confronted Karlstadt about his radical reforms. He quickly restored the Roman Mass with the exception of the references to sacrifice. Luther persisted with the concept of the "real presence" of Christ in the Eucharist. This led to a disagreement with Karlstadt, who was forced to retire and eventually banished from Saxony, feeling betrayed by Luther's backpedalling. Luther's appetite for reform had apparently slowed after his time in Wartburg Castle; he had emerged as a conservative. He kept much of the practices of the Catholic Church, including infant baptism, crucifixes, candles and altars. While teaching the doctrine of consubstantiation, in which Christ was really present but the bread was also really bread, he practised the Roman Mass which clearly expresses the doctrine of transubstantiation! This was confusing and may be pure semantics on Luther's part.

It is necessary to differentiate between the "early Luther", who was radical for change and the "Late Luther", who had been compromised by his alliance and dependence on the German princes. When challenged about infant baptism, he later replied: "Who is to say that babies have no faith?" "Late Luther" was really putting the brakes on and going into reverse. "Late Luther" also suggested that the earthly rulers should be the instrument of change in the Church. Those who ruled the land were regarded by Luther as ruling the Church. Here then was "Late Luther" appealing to the state to settle issues of faith.

In 1525, Luther also broke with Erasmus as a result of Erasmus' *Diatribe on Free Will*. This was countered by Luther's *Bondage of the Will* in which he stated his Augustinian view that man cannot will to turn to God or play any part in the process leading to his own salvation. Between 1525 and 1529, Luther carried on a controversy with Ulrich Zwingli regarding the Lord's Supper. Luther, while teaching consubstantiation, affirmed the Catholic view of transubstantiation by his practice, whereas Zwingli adopted a memorial view on the Lord's Supper.

During this period too, Luther had disputes with the radicals who felt that he had stopped short of major reforms. They felt bitterly disappointed. Instead of an explosion, they had witnessed a bang from a firecracker. Luther's Church was essentially Catholic in practice, only slightly sanitised. Instead of a Catholic Pope, there was now a Protestant Prophet. The German princes were satisfied with these cosmetic changes because they had ended up with the upper hand over the Church. State ruled the Church in Germany. Other princes in the rest of Europe must have looked on with envy.

Frederick the Wise of Saxony held the key to Luther's success, for without his support Luther could have been delivered into the hands of Emperor or Pope. Frederick had been the Pope's candidate in the election to the office of Emperor, which went instead to Charles V. He had a financial stake in the relics, the largest such collection in northern Germany, kept at the Castle Church, Wittenberg where Luther had nailed his Theses. Frederick's support of Luther was on the basis of his political opposition to the Emperor and his self-interest in not losing Luther, his most valuable asset from the University of Wittenberg, which he had founded. For Luther, throne and altar were still united. The Diet of Speyer saw an agreement for each area to adopt the religion of its German prince. Luther was unable to break out of the State/Church alliance and therefore was not able to restore the Church to a New Testament model.

The agreement hammered out at the Diet of Speyer shows Luther's understanding of the nature of the Church was similar to that of the Roman Catholic position. He still held the view of "Christian sacralism". For Luther, Christendom was still in existence except that his would be a Protestant one - perhaps slightly purer as far as Luther was concerned, but nevertheless still Christendom. This meant that mission and evangelism were unnecessary, as the faith of the people was determined by the faith of their princes. Religion was still imposed. When it was said therefore that Saxony, or Zurich, or Geneva had become Protestant, it was not through a preaching of the gospel and conversion; it had happened merely through the civil authorities in these places adopting these reforms and a chance to break from the control of Rome. Did they embrace the reforms out of conviction or were they motivated by nationalism? Was it spiritual or political? In the final analysis, were political considerations sometimes as important as spiritual convictions in these changes?

Luther's further dependence and alliance with the princes was demonstrated by his position in the Peasants' Revolts (1524-5). The demands of the peasants were summed up in the Twelve Articles of the Peasantry. They called for the congregational election of pastors, modification of tithes, abolition of serfdom, elimination of feudal taxes, discontinuing the enclosure of common land and reforming the administration of justice. Luther wrote a tract against them called Against the Murderous and Thieving Hordes of Peasants in harsh and uncompromising terms. He urged the princes to put down the revolt by turning the troops on the peasants. By April 1525 some 300,000 peasants were under arms. The forces of the Hesse, Saxon and Brunswick princes led to the peasants' defeat and Count Georg von Waldburg leading the Swabian League brutally crushed the peasant movement in Swabia, southern Germany.

The revolt was extremely detrimental to the Reformation. The disillusioned peasants turned against Luther and Lutheranism lost its popular appeal. It also enabled the princes to centralise their authority over their churches. The Catholics portrayed the revolt as a divine judgement against Protestantism.

How then should we view these early events of the Reformation? Undoubtedly Luther restored some vital aspects of the truth to the Church. Two things stand out in particular:

1) He brought the Church back to an evangelical faith by emphasising the authority of the Bible and justification by grace through faith. However, there was little in the way of evangelism because his understanding of the Church was still of a state-church variety, a Protestant Christendom.

2) Luther's removal of the papacy and its hierarchy was the start of a return to a simpler form of church government. The infallibility of the Pope and the doctrine of sacerdotalism were rejected. However, a Lutheran state-church which was part of the establishment soon had to create its own hierarchy. Hand in hand, the presbyters and the civil authorities created a Lutheran institution.

Apart from these two aspects, there was little in the way of recovery by Luther. There was no restoration of the pentecostal, and radical dimensions of the church. Luther's emphasis on faith and grace resulted in a devaluing of works among his followers.

Infant baptism was still in place. While consubstantiation was taught, the Roman Mass was still practised. Relics of Roman Catholicism were retained in its services. It is probably unfair to say that the changes seen in Lutheranism were merely cosmetic - the exchanging of a Catholic Pope for a Protestant Prophet. It is clear however that Luther did not go far enough. It was left to others to bring about further restoration and reforms.

Switzerland
Ulrich Zwingli (1484-1531)

Zwingli completed his studies at Basle where he came into contact with Erasmian humanism. He became a "Protestant" through reading the Greek New Testament a few years before Luther. In fact, the Reformation in Switzerland started spontaneously and took on its own characteristics. Like Luther then, it was again a return to the Scriptures that was responsible for Zwingli's faith and reforms.

The trigger for Luther's reforms was the sale of indulgences. For Zwingli it was the system of mercenary service in Italy. The Pope, along with many other Italian princes, had a professional army which used Swiss mercenaries. Even to this day, the Vatican has Swiss troops guarding it. Zwingli spoke out against this and in the process found himself attacking the whole papal system.

In 1518, he was called to be the priest at the Zurich Grossmunster largely because his views on the mercenary system were shared by an influential segment of the Zurich establishment. So strongly did the Zurich authorities feel about this issue that they were prepared to invite Zwingli despite fears by some that he was an Erasmian reformer. Between 1519 and 1525, Zwingli persuaded the city council that Zurich should become Protestant. The Mass was abolished and a practical programme of reform was instituted in co-operation with the magistrates. Zwingli was able to move beyond Luther and Erasmus to form his own Augustinian theology in the Swiss city-state. This was his version of Augustine's *City of God:* a Swiss Protestant State.

What was Zwingli's view of Church/State relationships? Like Luther, Zwingli had a "territorial concept" of the Church in which religion was imposed on the people by the State. Mission was through coercion rather than conversion. His views on the covenant and the Kingdom of God led Zwingli to identify the visible Church with the civil society. The Christian magistrates of such a city had the right to determine the external forms of the Church's worship and life and to govern the "Christian commonwealth" in co-operation with the prophet who expounded the Scriptures.

While on the nature of the Church Zwingli moved no further than Luther, he did break with Luther over the issue of the Eucharist: instead of the "real presence" of Christ in the Eucharist, Zwingli for a time taught that the Lord's Supper was merely a memorial with no spiritual benefits whatsoever. This was an overreaction. He had gone from a high view of the Mass to a low view of the Eucharist. This he was later to modify and came to a view which was closer to a doctrine of spiritual presence.

In October 1523, he broke with his radical followers led by Conrad Grebel and Felix Manz whom he viewed as a threat to public order. Grebel and Manz had been studying the Bible with Zwingli and had initially supported his reforms. Zwingli at first advocated believer's baptism. But when Zwingli reversed his earlier convictions and bowed to the Zurich authorities over the speed of reform and infant baptism, Grebel and Manz broke with him and found themselves the target of persecution by their former friend. These "Anabaptists" (re-baptisers) would have endangered Zwingli's alliance with the magistrate whose support he believed was essential to implement the reforms. Tragically Zwingli personally approved the drowning of Manz in Lake Zurich in 1527. There were earlier executions of Anabaptists, but this was the first in Zurich.

Recent scholarship has shown that many of the early Anabaptists such as Reublin and Hubmaier agreed with Zwingli's understanding of the State Church. It was only after the Schleitheim Confession of 1527 that the Swiss Brethren agreed to a separation of Church and State. The dispute between Zwingli and the Swiss Brethren therefore had more to do with the speed of the reforms and eventually with infant baptism than with the Church/State issue.

Zwingli's last years were marked by increasing political activity. Although the urban cantons of Basle, Schaffhausen, Bern and Constance had accepted Zwingli's reforms, others had not. This led to a two-year war with the Forest Cantons. In 1531 Zwingli was himself killed fighting at the battle of Kappel. In a sense this was inevitable. If religion has to be imposed by coercion using the powers of the State, the Church would invariably become embroiled in the political activities of the State. Like Luther then, Zwingli died with the blood of men on his hands.

John Calvin (1509-1564)

Calvin was a Frenchman who studied law initially at Orleans and then in Paris. Like Luther and Zwingli before him, he was converted through studying the Greek New Testament under Melchior Wolmar, a humanist with strong Protestant leanings. As a young man, Calvin became one of the leaders of secret Protestant meetings in Paris. It has been said that he had the most brilliant theological mind since Augustine.

At the age of 23, Calvin helped his friend Nicholas Cop prepare his inaugural address as the new rector of Paris University. The address was a strong attack on the Catholic Church and demanded reforms along the lines advocated by Luther. It resulted in an explosion of anti-Protestant feeling and both Cop and Calvin had to flee Paris. Calvin was to spend the next three years wandering through France, Switzerland and Italy.

Despite his wanderings, Calvin began his writings. He wrote *Psychopannychia* (1534) to attack the doctrine of soul sleep after death. In the same year, Olivetan's French translation of the Bible was published with a preface by Calvin. In Basle in 1536, aged 27, he published a slim volume of seven chapters called *Institutes of the Christian Religion*. This book, which he published later in several expanded editions, was to be Calvin's most famous work and became popular among Protestants as both an able exposition and apology for the new doctrines. Still fleeing from one place to another, Calvin arrived in Geneva. When Guillaume Farel, the Protestant preacher, heard of his presence, he insisted that Calvin should stay and help him implement reforms in the city. His residence here was not to be long. He and Farel sought to introduce into a highly immoral city a measure of strict Christian rules and discipline. Opposition meant both men had to flee Geneva.

Calvin went to Strasbourg at the invitation of Martin Bucer to pastor the French refugee congregation along New Testament lines. These were probably Calvin's happiest years. He married Idelette de Bure, a widow of an Anabaptist whom he had led to conversion. He drew up a liturgy and started preparing his commentary on Romans, as well as engaging in theological debates as a representative of Strasbourg.

In 1541, the government of Geneva fell into the hands of Calvin's friends, who persuaded him to return. He was to stay 20 years until his death. Calvin's aim was to make Geneva a "holy city", the same vision as Augustine and following in the footsteps of Zwingli. He wanted a city conformed to the will of God. This meant a strict discipline of which most did not approve, especially the inhabitants who were not Calvinists. Even the Calvinists felt that at times he carried his demands too far. The result was occasional riots and disturbances.

Many visitors arrived to see the reforms taking place. One such was Michael Servetus, a Spaniard under sentence of death by the Catholic Inquisition for apparently being anti-Trinitarian. He was arrested by Calvin with the approval of the Swiss city and the Roman Catholic authorities and burnt at the stake in 1553, not with dry wood, but with green wood so that it would burn more slowly prolonging death. Calvin's part in this horrendous act demonstrated that his understanding of state-church relationships was no different from the Catholics, Luther or Zwingli - Church must govern the State. Servetus' doctrines included rejection of the papacy, transubstantiation and infant baptism, whilst advocating freedom of conscience and evangelism to the Muslims and Jews. Whether he was anti-Trinitarian or had difficulties expressing the Trinity was never substantiated.

Geneva under Calvin went further than either Luther or Zwingli. The churches were devoid of crucifixes,images and altars. There were no organs either! He instituted the presbyterian system of church government using a body of laymen and pastors to govern the churches. It became a model Protestant city and soon was a haven for other Protestant refugees. It was estimated that 6,000 out of a population of 13,000 were refugees from France, Holland, England, Scotland, Germany, Italy, Spain and Hungary. These were all influenced by Calvin and carried the Calvinist reforms and doctrines when they returned. Calvin became the dominant figure of the Protestant reformation in the middle of the 16th century.

France was one of the countries which was initially influenced by Calvin. Protestants there were called Huguenots and experienced rapid growth. Then on August 24, St Bartholomew's day, 1572, 22,000 were massacred by the Catholic authorities - 2,000 in Paris alone. The Huguenots fled to England, Holland and Geneva. However, the country most influenced by Geneva was Scotland. Patrick Hamilton was one of those burnt as a heretic for advocating the reforms of Luther and Calvin. In 1559 however, John Knox, the preacher at St Andrew's Castle, was finally able to persuade the Scottish parliament to "become" Protestant.

****

It is often claimed that Luther, Zwingli and Calvin should be understood in the context of their time. They were a product of their age and were limited in their vision. While there is of course some merit to this argument, it is not sufficient to excuse their shortcomings. Consider:

1) The Reformers had the Bible. The problem was that they were selective about what truths they embraced and rejected. We all suffer from this tunnel-vision approach to God's Word. It is one

thing to get a hold of God's Word. It is something else to allow God's Word to get a hold of us.

2) The Reformers had the writings of the Early Church Fathers. There were examples there that would have led them back to a New Testament understanding of the Church. Again they were selective about what they learnt from church history. They were comfortable with Augustine, whose writings were readily available, but do not appear to have read Tertullian very carefully. Are we any different today? In addition, they had the history of the radical protest movements to learn from, had they wished so to do.

3) They had contemporaries who spoke out against their shortcomings and excesses. Erasmus and the Anabaptists spoke out against the use of force for conversion. The Anabaptists challenged the Reformers concerning the "territorial" state-churches they were creating as well as their views on believers' baptism and mission.

4) The fundamental weakness about all three Reformers was their inability to separate Church from State. Much of the defects and suffering from the Reformation can be traced to this basic issue. So long as the Church was in league with the State, it would always be a part of the establishment. It would always be corrupted by the world and tempted to use the ways of the world as well as the machinery of the State to enforce the faith and build an earthly kingdom. This separatist stance was hard for 16th century people to conceptualise - even the Anabaptists struggled to see it.

The most honest excuse is that the Reformers were men of their time. They were trying to reform the Church as responsibly as they knew how, and they viewed a separation of Church and State as a recipe for chaos and disaster. They also, like the rest of us, were given over to prejudices, fear and pride. We should not over-glorify them neither should we dismiss them completely. Rather, we should see them as playing a role in the purposes of God to bring the Church back to its roots. A better way was yet to come.

12

THE CATHOLIC REFORMATION

By 1580, 60 years after Luther, Protestantism had spread to Germany, Denmark, Norway, Sweden, England, Scotland and Switzerland. But most of Ireland, a good part of France, Spain, Italy, Austria, Switzerland and Germany remained Catholic. The boundaries stayed the same for the next 300 years and are still largely the same today. Why did the Reformation stop after 60 years?

The answer was twofold: First, the agreement forged at the Diet of Speyer placed a real constraint on evangelism. A Catholic prince ruling a Catholic population was a closed door to Protestant evangelism. The only way in which the boundaries of Protestantism could be enlarged was through political means - either military annexation or appealing to the political benefits of independence from Rome. Most Reformed Churches had little mission focus in any case and would not have been able to take up opportunities had they existed. Second, there was the Counter Reformation. The attack on Rome had robbed the Catholic Church of half of Europe. Rome would not sit by doing nothing. Rome did three things that helped stop the spread of Protestantism:

1) A Roman Catholic counterpart to Martin Luther called Ignatius Loyola was raised up. A Spanish nobleman who had a vision of God while recovering from war wounds in hospital, Loyola felt a specific call to stop the spread of Protestantism. He started

the *Society of Jesus*, or Jesuits, in Paris with a group of six other noblemen. Loyola had a large following and subjected his followers to "spiritual exercises" for 30 days including fasting, prayer and the meditation of Scripture. After this rigorous training, they were ready to become Jesuits. One of their tasks was to keep Europe for Rome and on the whole they were successful, not least because of the excellence of the education which they provided for European noblemen. The Jesuits established orphanages, houses for reclaiming prostitutes, schools, centres of poor relief and even a system of banking for the destitute peasants. Unlike the Protestants, the Jesuits were a force for mission. Outstanding among them was Francis Xavier who almost single-handed brought about the conversion of 700,000 people to Catholic Christianity in India, the East Indies and Japan.

2) The Pope called the Council of Trent which met some 25 times between 1545 and 1563. Although the Pope had initially wanted to have dialogue with the Protestants, he was dissuaded from doing so by his cardinals. Among other things, the Council of Trent stated the following:

- The curse of God was pronounced on all Protestants.

- There were seven sacraments, not two, and these were all necessary for salvation.

- Tradition must be placed alongside Scriptures.

- The Apocrypha must be part of the Bible.

- Purgatory did exist and it was heretical to deny it.

- Indulgences, invocation of saints, images, and relics are pious practices.

- The Pope had absolute authority.

This was the first time these doctrines had been clearly stated by Rome. They have not changed since then and cannot because the Council cannot err. The Second Vatican Council in 1962 has softened on some of these issues and it is clear that many

Catholics, including theologians, disagree with them. The decrees told the Catholics what they believed so that they could answer Protestants.

3) The Inquisition was revived and was used against Protestants and Anabaptists in Spain, Italy and parts of Austria and Germany. This had the effect of wiping out Protestants from these places so, that even today, they are a small minority.

These three activities together helped to put a stop to the spread of Protestantism in Europe. The Counter-Reformation did bring necessary reforms to the Catholic Church. The power of the papacy and the abuses of the Pope were also reined in. Attempts were made to stamp out the corruption of the hierarchy. There was also a genuine attempt, in part educational and in part almost evangelistic, to spread a renewed Catholic spirituality. All these factors made Catholicism more acceptable and attractive, and discouraged further defections to the Protestants.

13

THE RADICAL REFORMATION

These radical groups have variously been called "the Stepchildren" of the Reformation or the left-wing of the Reformation, and what they founded were often known as Believers' Churches. They were, however, popularly known as Anabaptists because of their emphasis on believers' baptism. For them, the Protestant Reformation had turned into a disappointment because of the compromises and concessions made to the civil rulers in order to establish the reforms. Instead of a "big bang", the Reformation was only a "little pop" for these radicals. They were deeply disillusioned by what seemed to them to be the Reformers' backtracking on many issues regarding the nature of the church and faith. The Reformers' appeal to the State in matters of faith and practice showed that they had not moved from a territorial state-church concept. Their backtracking on believers' baptism only re-inforced this view. Those who were originally close to Zwingli particularly felt betrayed, given his earlier views.

Until recently, it was believed that the early beginnings of the Anabaptists were solely among the Swiss Brethren. It is now accepted however, that Anabaptism spontaneously sprang up in three places at almost the same time - Switzerland, southern Germany and the Netherlands. But the earliest of these groups were the Swiss Brethren, who emerged in 1525 in the city and canton of Zurich. They were the first to articulate these principles and witness to them with their lives. Fritz Blanke, commenting on the first and tragically short-lived Anabaptist congregation in Zollikon, near Zurich, said: "In Zollikon, a new type of church had begun to differentiate itself, the Free Church type. Zollikon is the cradle for this idea, which from here entered upon its triumphal march through four centuries and through the whole world." And again:

> "The decision of Conrad Grebel to refuse to accept the jurisdiction of the Zurich council over the Zurich church is one of the high moments of history, for however obscure it was, it marked the beginning of the modern 'free church' movement."
> (Harold Bender)

It was left to the Radical Reformers to recover the truth about the nature of the Church and to live out the radical lifestyle of true discipleship. The price paid to restore these truths to the Church was higher than that paid by Luther, Zwingli or Calvin. Perhaps Satan knew that more than the Reformation, the Radical Reformation was going to pose an even greater threat to his kingdom. By their willingness to use the sword for conversion, the Reformers had used the instrument of the enemy. The Reformers were tainted by the world's system and were concentrating on building an earthly kingdom. Satan could accommodate that. But these radicals were something else. They refused to use the earthly sword - only the sword of the Spirit. They worked for the separation of State and Church. They demanded to see signs of repentance and faith before baptism. They emphasised practical love and experienced brotherhood in new ways. They were passionate about mission. They walked the way of peace as Jesus did. They were dangerous. Was this why, above all other groups, they were the most persecuted?

In wanting to go further than the Reformers, the Anabaptists found themselves facing two enemies - Catholics and Protestants. Whereas the Protestant Reformers had only the Catholic authorities to worry about, these radicals had two, both prepared to use violence against them. In a sense, the Anabaptists were easier prey. Unlike the Protestants, the radicals had no political or military powers to defend them. They were totally vulnerable and threw themselves on the mercy of God for protection. Nevertheless, they seemed dangerous because they were calling into question the very structures of Christendom.

Switzerland
Conrad Grebel, Felix Manz and Georg Blaurock

Ulrich Zwingli, with his push for reforms, was able to attract a group of young scholars including Conrad Grebel (1495-1526) and Felix Manz (?1498-1527), who met regularly to study the Bible. They came to the view that transubstantiation, infant baptism and the union of State and Church were erroneous. They placed Scripture above traditions and believed the Bible to be their final arbiter of truth. Again we see what a dangerous practice it is for believers to meet together to study the Bible! They would see truths which would demand obedience. Here was a group that was willing to submit traditions and beliefs to be tested by the Scriptures.

Obedience to the Word had a price. In December 1523, Zwingli was forced by the city council to back down on his reforms of the Mass, thus indicating that the State had the authority over matters of faith and practice in the Church. Despite Zwingli's biblical convictions, he could see no other model than the union of State and Church - corpus Christianum. Some of his followers were deeply disappointed. Grebel, Manz and others began meeting privately to discuss and study the Bible in order to arrive at the truth. They wrote to other Evangelical reformers including Sebastian Munster at the University of Basle, and Karlstadt, Luther's associate, seeking guidance. They believed that obedience to biblical teachings involved rejection of infant baptism and adoption of believers' baptism. Two Zurich priests associated with the group, William Reublin and John Brotli, stopped baptising the children of their parishioners. On January 18, 1525, the city council ruled that anyone refusing infant baptism for their children would be expelled from the canton. Interestingly, they also banned independent Bible study groups - the authorities knew where these radical ideas were coming from.

Although baptism had not been the initial issue, it became the symbol of the opposing church view. The trigger for the Reformation of Luther was the sale of indulgences; for Zwingli it was the Pope's mercenary army. For the Anabaptists it was going to be baptism. In the face of the ultimatum from the city council, 12 men gathered on the evening of January 21, 1525, at the home of Manz to decide what should be done. Among them was George Blaurock, a priest from Chur, who

> "arose after prayer and asked Conrad Grebel to baptise him, for the sake of God, with the true Christian baptism upon his faith and knowledge. And when he knelt down with that request and desire, Conrad baptised him, since at that time there was no ordained servant to perform such works. After that was done the others similarly desired George to baptise them, which he also did upon their request . . . Each confirmed the other in the service of the gospel, and they began to teach and keep the faith."

This service marked the beginnings of the Radical Reformation. Manz endured several imprisonments but led many to join the Anabaptists through his quiet testimony. He was the first Anabaptist to die at the hands of a Protestant government, although others had been killed by Catholic authorities before him. He was drowned in the Limmat River in Zurich on January 5, 1527, as a macabre play on the practice of "re-baptism". He was only 29. Grebel was one of the few early leaders who did not die a violent death. Weakened by his imprisonment, he died of plague less than two years after the first baptism, aged 28.

Blaurock (c.1492-1529) founded the first Anabaptist congregation at Zollikon where he won more than 150 converts with his powerful preaching. The authorities arrested him and he was exiled from Zurich in 1527. He became an itinerant evangelist, winning thousands to Christ and planting Anabaptist churches over much of Central Europe. Many congregations were established in the Austrian Tyrol which afterwards supplied thousands of members for Anabaptist colonies in Moravia. Hapsburg officials caught Blaurock in the end and burnt him for heresy. He was 37.

Germany
Balthasar Hubmaier (?1481-1528) and Hans Denck

William Reublin travelled to the Swiss German border near Waldshut where Dr Balthasar Hubmaier, a learned theologian, was priest. Like Zwingli, his friend, Hubmaier had come to question infant baptism on biblical grounds. Unlike Zwingli though, he was prepared to go further. Hubmaier was baptised by Reublin in April 1525 along with 60 members of his congregation. On Easter Sunday, he himself baptised 300 of his parishioners, including his wife. This was the first case of an entire congregation joining the Anabaptists. The Catholic authorities quickly retaliated. Hubmaier and his wife lost everything as they escaped from an advancing Austrian army. They reached Zurich but were soon discovered by Zwingli's Protestant government and thrown into prison. The Zurich Council arranged a debate between Hubmaier and Zwingli in which Hubmaier, weakened by imprisonment, was overwhelmed by his robust opponent. Fearful of being handed over to the Emperor, Hubmaier retracted some of his teaching, but immediately repented bitterly of his fear of man and sought God's forgiveness and restoration.

On his release from prison, he went to Constance, then to Augsburg, where he baptised Hans Denck. He then travelled to Nikolsburg in Moravia, subsequently known as the "America of the 16th century" because of the tolerant policy of some of its landowner nobles. He busied himself with writing, publishing 16 books, and became the most prolific literary protagonist of the Anabaptist cause. He was finally arrested by the imperial forces of King Ferdinand in 1528, taken to Vienna where he was burnt at the stake. His dying prayer was:

"Oh my gracious God, give me patience in martyrdom. Oh my Father, I thank Thee that Thou wilt take me today out of this vale of sorrow. Oh Lamb, Lamb, who takest away the sin of the world. Oh my God, into Thy hands I commit my spirit." From the flames he was heard to cry out: "Jesus, Jesus!"

Three days later, his heroic wife Elsbeth was executed by drowning in the Danube. Hubmaier was killed but his message lived on. "Truth was immortal" was one of his favourite sayings.

Hans Denck (c.1495-1527), a native of Bavaria, was another of the influential leaders of the movement. He studied in Basle and was appointed in 1523 to one of the most important schools in Nuremberg, where the Lutheran reformation had been under way for a year under the young and gifted Andreas Osiander. Forced to leave Nuremberg in 1525 because of his "horrible error", Denck became a wanderer throughout southern Germany. He spent a year in Augsburg, where he was baptised by the visiting Hubmaier. The church here grew to 11,000 members by 1527. Church growth was not new to these radicals. As a result of persecution, Denck left Augsburg and took refuge in Strasbourg where there was also a large assembly of baptised believers. The leaders of the Protestant party were Capito and Bucer, who were not committed to either Luther or Zwingli, though Zwingli's introduction of capital punishment for religious deviants weakened his influence with Capito. Denck soon became friendly with Capito and his godliness, ability and personal charm drew many to him. However, Bucer, in conjunction with Zwingli and the city council, soon arranged an expulsion order. Denck had to move on once again. He was also an evangelist among the Jewish communities along the Rhine. In Worms, Germany, where there was also a large congregation, Denck printed the edition of the Old Testament prophetic books which he and Ludwig Hetzer had translated from the Hebrew. Denck also took part in the "Martyrs' Conference" in Augsburg where he opposed many who advocated the use of force against the growing persecution. He died of the plague in Basle in November 1527. He was in his early thirties.

Michael Sattler (c.1490-1527)

Michael Sattler was one of the dominant figures of the Anabaptist movement. He was a prior in a monastery outside Freiburgim-Breisgau but had become an Anabaptist under the influence of William Reublin in Zurich. After the death of Felix Manz, Sattler emerged as the most able leader among Swiss German Anabaptists. No other Anabaptist leader remained active in the area - Hubmaier was in Moravia, Blaurock was in the Tyrol, and Denck was evangelising along the Rhine. By this time, Grebel and Manz were both dead.

With the loss of leadership by execution, there was a danger of excesses and errors which could have diverted the movement. A conference was called in February 1527 with Michael Sattler playing a vital role. The *Schleitheim Confession* was agreed. This was really a "brotherly accord", a list of things that the diverse leaders who gathered there came to an agreement over. It made several declarations:

1) Baptism	Only for those "who have learned repentance and amendment of life and who walk in the resurrection of Jesus Christ", that is, only believers should be baptised.
2) Ban	Discipline should be exercised in the Church, with the exclusion from fellowship of disorderly members.
3) Lord's Supper	"All those who wish to drink of one drink as a remembrance of the shed blood of Christ shall be united beforehand by baptism .. ."
4) Separation	"the command of the Lord is clear when he calls upon us to be separated from the evil, that is, the world..."
5) Pastors	They should be elected by the congregations and not chosen by bishops or princes. The duty of the shepherd was to "teach, admonish, to lead in prayer, to lift up the bread, and in all things to see to the care of the body of Christ... " They should be "one who out-and-out has a good report of those who are outside the faith".

6) Sword	Christians should not use the sword or go to law. "In the Law, the sword was ordained for the punishment of the wicked .. . and the same is ordained to be used by the worldly magistrate." The Anabaptists agreed that the sword was "outside the perfection of Christ" and thus could not be wielded by Christians whether in private or worldly functions, although those outside Christ's perfection (that is, non-Christians) might be expected to use it. On the whole, they taught that a Christian could not be a soldier or a magistrate, because it involved the use of violence.
7) Oath	"Christ, who teaches the perfection of the Law, prohibits all swearing to his followers, whether true or false."

On his return from Schleitheim to Horb, Sattler was arrested and nine charges were laid against him. These are listed because they provide an insight into the testimony of the Anabaptists:

- That he and his adherents acted contrary to the decree of the Emperor.

- He taught, maintained and believed that the body and blood of Christ were not present in his sacrament.

- He taught and believed that infant baptism was not efficacious for salvation.

- He rejected the sacrament of extreme unction.

- They despised and reviled the Mother of God, and condemned the saints.

- He declared that men should not swear before a magistrate.

- He has commenced a new and unheard of custom in regard to the Lord's Supper, placing the bread and the wine on a plate, eating and drinking the same.

- Contrary to the rule, he has taken a wife.

- He said if the Turks invaded the country, we ought not to resist them, and if he approved of war, he would rather take the field against the Christians than against the Turks, not withstanding, it is an important matter to set the greatest enemies of our faith against us.

Although Sattler's defence was both skilful and courageous, he was found guilty and sentenced to death on the May 18, 1527. The execution of Sattler became the most well known of any 16th-century Anabaptist. This was because the authorities wanted to make an example of Sattler and his trial was carried out over two days. It was a case of kill one to frighten ten thousand, or so they thought. Sattler was subjected to prolonged torture and then burned alive. Four accounts of the death of Sattler and his faithful wife are available. His courageous defence and valiant death created a boomerang effect that had not been anticipated. "Perhaps no other martyrdom of an Anabaptist so publicised the faith and faithfulness of Anabaptists to a German-speaking audience"(Estep). The story of his trial and death is moving and worthy of quoting here:

"The torture, a prelude to the execution, began at the market place, where a piece was cut from Sattler's tongue. Pieces of flesh were torn from his body twice with red-hot tongs. He was then tied to a cart. On the way to the execution he was burned with the tongs five more times. At the site of the execution, still able to speak, Sattler prayed for his persecutors. They tied him to a ladder and pushed him into the fire. He admonished the people, the judges and the mayor to repent and be converted. Then he prayed: "Almighty eternal God, Thou art the Way and the Truth; because I have not been shown to be in error, I will with Thy help to this day testify to the truth and seal it with my blood." When the ropes on his wrists had burned, Sattler raised both forefingers, giving the promised signal to his fellow Anabaptists that a martyr's death was bearable. Then he was heard to pray: "Father, I commend my spirit into Thy hands.""

He was 37. Sattler's faithful wife, Margareta, was drowned eight days later in the Neckar river. Lutherans, Reformed and even Catholic witnesses were never quite able to forget the scene of that infamous day in Rottenberg. Both Bucer and Capito were grieved and shaken. This was a significant event in the advancement of Anabaptism. Rather than frightening the believers, Sattler's martyrdom served to strengthen the resolve of the Anabaptists to stay true to their Lord. No amount of cruelty and torture could hold back the longing of these believers to understand and live out the truth as revealed in God's Word. If Luther could say: "My conscience is captive to the Word of God", the Anabaptists would add: "Our conscience and our bodies are captive to the Word of God".

Thousands died for their faith. What was particularly striking was that many of the leaders died young. Manz was 29, Grebel 28, Blaurock 37, Denck 35(?) and Sattler 37. I have entered three dates into my diary each year to remind me of the price that others have paid for my faith: October 31 reminds me of the nailing of Luther's Ninety-five Theses, the January 21 of the first re-baptism of the Anabaptists and May 18 the death of Michael Sattler, who paid so dearly for his love of the Lord.

Eastern Europe
Jakob Hutter and the Hutterites

With increased persecution, Anabaptists were forced to move and some found asylum in Moravia, where the nobles had a long tradition of independence in both religious and political matters. There were two separate groups that gathered at Nikolsburg which became the centre of Anabaptism in Moravia.

The first group was led by Hubmaier, who maintained that a Christian could be a magistrate and that defensive war was permissible. This group was given the nickname "men of the sword" (Schwertler). The other group was led by Jacob ("One-eyed Jacob") Widemann, a product of John Hut's fiery eschatology. He condemned mingling of Church and State and advocated non-resistance. They were called the "men of the staff" (Stabler). The issue of war was at the forefront because of the impending threat of Turkish invasion. The two groups were unable to reconcile their differences and went their separate ways.

Wiedemann led his group to Austerlitz in 1529 and founded the first Bruderhof, or colony of brothers, as a formal community. This was to become the distinguishing mark of the movement. Wiedemann was autocratic and the movement would not have survived but for the efforts of Jacob Hutter (d.1536), named after his hatmaking trade. Born in South Tyrol, Hutter became the leading figure in Austrian Anabaptism after the execution of Blaurock. He heard of the religious freedom in Moravia and went there first to investigate possible resettlement of his persecuted Austrian followers. His organisational skills and piety allowed him to restore order and a measure of unity to the Bruderhof. He put the Bruderhof at Austerlitz on a firm economic footing. It is a credit to his leadership that these Anabaptists chose to be named after him even though he was not their founder.

Following the Munster debacle (see later), the Austrians put renewed pressure on the Moravian nobles to persecute the Anabaptists. The Hutterites were forced to leave their Bruderhofs. Hutter returned to the Tyrol where he was immediately arrested and burnt at the stake in February 1536. His pregnant wife escaped but was later captured and killed.

There was no peace for the Hutterites wandering around Moravia until 1555, with the signing of the *Peace of Augsburg*. From 1565 until the end of the century they enjoyed a "golden period" of peace and growth. Under the able leadership of men such as Peter Walpot (1518-78) and Peter Riedemann (1506-66), they founded some 100 Bruderhofs with a total membership of 30,000 - 70,000. Each Bruderhof was a self-sufficient community, where the community of goods was practised. Men and women were assigned to work according to their abilities. Children were cared for in nurseries. An excellent school system was established. The Hutterites are said to have had complete literacy, a remarkable achievement for that day and place.

In 1605, the Turks invaded Moravia, destroying 16 colonies and devastating the rest. The Catholic Reformation also caught up with them in the person of the persecuting Cardinal von Dietrichstein after the battle of the White Mountain in 1620. By 1622, all Protestants in Moravia had been killed, driven out or forcibly converted to Catholicism. The Hutterite survivors, probably 1,000 in all, retreated to Slovakia and Transylvania where they existed for 150 years. Repeated persecutions forced them to move into Walachia (modern-day Romania) and eventually to Russia in 1770 where they flourished. The introduction of military service in 1870 by the Tsar, despite his earlier promises to the contrary, forced them to emigrate again, this time to South Dakota in the New World where they settled. The traditional Hutterites have survived in considerable numbers in the great plains of the United States and Canada, where they live in self-governing agricultural communities.

Holland

Munster Disaster

Jan Matthys and John of Leyden were two firebrand Dutch immigrants who arrived in Munster, Westphalia, preaching a fanatical vision of the New Jerusalem which was to be established in the city. The citizens were forced into baptism or were expelled on pain of death. In response, the city was laid under siege by the armies of the Catholic bishop. During this time, community of goods was enforced. Citizens were forced to bring their goods to a central store and food rationing was introduced. New laws were introduced to suit the "New Israel" including polygamy. John of Leyden was proclaimed king of the whole earth to make known the kingdom of the New Zion. Along with others of the day, they believed in the imminent return of the Lord. In 1521 Luther had announced that the end would come in 1524 and rushed the publication of the book of Daniel before the rest of his Old Testament translation:

> "There was present an apocalypticism and a messianism, with hallucinations thrown in"(Verduin).

The forces of the Catholic bishop of Munster finally crushed the rebellion and most of the inhabitants of the city were slaughtered. It was a major aberration and was used as an excuse for the increased persecution of the Anabaptists. The whole episode discredited the Anabaptists who had spoken and written against the fanaticism at Munster. The great historian Arnold Toynbee has said: "Munster was a caricature of the movement". The main factor behind the Munster Disaster was the concept of an earthly kingdom, the "City of God" that could be enforced by violence. In this view, they were no different to the Reformers or the Catholic Church. This was a far cry from the ideals of the Anabaptists but regrettably this disaster would be used for centuries as the basis for further accusations of heresy against them.

Menno Simons (1496-1561)

Menno Simons was the Dutch Anabaptist pastor who constructed his theological works after the Munster tragedy. He was born in Friesland and though he was a Catholic priest started reading the writings of Luther and other reformers before becoming an Anabaptist in 1536. Even before his death in 1561, the Anabaptists in the Netherlands were often referred to as Mennonites. Such was his influence and teachings that he was hounded from place to place. Charles V, Emperor of the Holy Roman Empire, published an edict against him and placed a price of 100 guilders on his head. Menno Simons laboured for two years around Amsterdam with good success. Those baptised were often executed but he somehow avoided capture himself. Amazingly he found time to write three books during this period of his ministry in northern Holland.

In 1543, he left Holland for the more tolerant religious climate of northern Germany. He spent the next 18 years there until his death. His writings were voluminous and eventually translated into many languages including English. He was called the "Theologian of the New Birth" because of his emphasis on the necessity of being born again. In 1609-1612, Menno's writings were to have a strong influence on John Smyth and his followers, the group to whom the English Baptists trace their beginnings.

14

THE ENGLISH REFORMATION

The English Reformation was a typical English compromise between Rome and the Protestant Reformers. Political expediency as much as religious conviction seems to have been the main force behind the Reformation in England.

King Henry VIII, on the issue of a papal dispensation in 1509, chose to marry Catherine of Aragon, his brother's widow, thus continuing an alliance between the Tudors and the Spanish throne. Shortly after the appearance of Luther's tracts of 1520, Henry VIII wrote a treatise called *Defence of the Seven Sacraments* which so impressed the Pope that he was granted the title "Defender of the Faith". Henry was concerned with his inability to produce a male heir to the throne. All the babies his wife bore were stillborn except Mary, who was to be the Queen stigmatised by Protestants as "Bloody Mary". Through his leading minister, Thomas Wolsey, he applied to the Pope for an annulment of his marriage to Catherine. This was refused.

Henry then proceeded to remove Wolsey from office in 1529 and began his assault on papal control in England. With the death of Archbishop Warham and the resignation of Lord Chancellor Sir Thomas More, Henry moved quickly. Thomas Cranmer was named Archbishop of Canterbury; the annulment was granted. This was only the first of four marriages which he would help Henry to unscramble. Henry and Anne Boleyn were secretly married by Cranmer.

Parliament, under the guidance of Thomas Cromwell, began to pass a series of laws that placed England outside the sphere of Rome's control. Appeals to Rome were forbidden, Peter's Pence (a compulsory levy of one penny per household to Rome) was stopped, and the clergy were required to submit to the throne. Needing money to support his kingdom, Henry seized the wealthy monasteries and sold off the land to individuals, creating new wealth for the gentry and merchant classes. There were protests, and More and John Fisher, the Bishop of Rochester, both friends of Erasmus, were executed.

The succession still was unsettled for want of a son. Anne Boleyn was accused of adultery and beheaded. Next day, Henry married Jane Seymour, who did produce a son, the future Edward VI but 12 days later she died. In 1540 Henry was enticed by Cromwell into marrying Anne of Cleves, who was a Protestant. Upon her arrival he was so displeased with her that the marriage was not consummated and was dissolved. He next married Catherine Howard, later charged with adultery and beheaded in 1542. Finally he married Catherine Parr, who survived him. Cromwell fell from grace as a result of the Anne of Cleves episode and was beheaded.

With the Act of Supremacy in 1534, Henry repudiated the authority of the Pope and declared himself head of the Church of England. Henry had intended to do little more than replace the Pope with himself; he wanted an English Catholic Church instead of a Roman Catholic Church. Henry remained basically a Catholic unwilling to subscribe to many Protestant doctrines - but then he had not reckoned with the likes of Tyndale, Cranmer, Cromwell and Latimer.

William Tyndale (c.1494-1536) was educated at Oxford and Cambridge. He became convinced that

"it was impossible to establish the lay people in any truth, except the Scripture were plain laid before their eyes in their mother tongue".

Finding no support at all, he left England, never to return. The printing of his New Testament in English was begun in 1525 in Cologne, but a raid by papal agents stopped the work, and it had to be completed in Worms. Tyndale's output in terms of his Bible translations and theological work was impressive, especially considering the conditions under which he worked. He was hounded from place to place, and shipwrecked with loss of manuscripts. Secret agents were sent after him by William Warham, the Archbishop of Canterbury. Police raids were carried out on his printer and he was betrayed by friends. He was finally arrested and imprisoned in Vilvorde near Brussels in 1535, before being strangled and burnt. Tyndale never completed translating the whole Bible. His work was completed by Coverdale. One copy of his Bible was later to be placed in every church in England. Thomas Cranmer, Archbishop of Canterbury (1489-1556) was also steadily becoming a convinced Protestant. The Six Articles (1539) marked a return by Henry to Catholic doctrine, as perhaps did his marriage to Catherine Howard. He decreed the death penalty for anyone denying the doctrine of transubstantiation. By 1545, Nicholas Ridley, the Bishop of London, had been convinced of the error of transubstantiation, and the following year he persuaded Cranmer who in turn won over Hugh Latimer, Bishop of Worcester (1485-1555). It was said at Ridley's trial in 1553 that "Latimer leaneth to Cranmer, Cranmer to Ridley, and Ridley to the singularity of his own wit". As Bishop of London, Ridley was to take the lead in the removal of stone altars and the substitution of wooden communion tables.

Cranmer wisely bided his time. His opportunity as a reformer came under Edward VI (1547-53), when the two successive protectors of England - the dukes of Somerset and Northumberland - were committed to reform. Developments were fast and furious with the accession of Edward, aged ten, to the throne. Several things happened then:

1) The services were now to be celebrated in English rather than Latin.

2) Cranmer wrote his two versions of the Book of Common Prayers for everyone to use. Ridley helped with the compilation of 1549 and its revision in 1552.

3) The clergy were allowed to marry. It transpired that Cranmer had secretly married in the 1530s.

4) The altar was now called the Lord's table, taking on a Protestant character.

5) Every priest had to preach at least four times a year, giving English people an insight into the state of the clergy.

6) The *Articles of Faith* was published, setting the tone for Protestantism in England.

During Edward VI's brief reign, refugees began to return from Europe. Martin Bucer, the reformer from Strasbourg visited Cambridge where he taught the students the Protestant gospel.

The people of England were still getting to grips with the changes when the pendulum swung back again after the death of the boy king, aged 16, after only six years' reign. In 1553 his half-sister, Mary, came to the throne determined to make England Roman Catholic again. 1,200 clergy who had married were either dismissed or told to separate from their wives. Parliament was made to kneel to the cardinal from Rome to be received back into the Catholic Church. The Latin Mass was restored and from 1555 to 1558, Protestants were regularly burnt - nearly 300 in three years. The number was not great compared with those who lost their lives for their faith in other European countries, but it exceeded all the executions for heresy under Henry VIII. The basis was laid for the long-lasting anti-Catholic hysteria and earned a lasting name for the Queen, Bloody Mary. Among those burned as heretics during her reign were Latimer, Ridley, John Hooper (Bishop of Gloucester) and Archbishop Cranmer. He had recanted his views under pressure, though he repented of this before his death.

Elizabeth I (1533-1603) came to the throne in 1558, succeeding her Roman Catholic sister when England was both divided and defenceless. She was an illegitimate child as far as the Pope was concerned, being a daughter of Henry VIII and Anne Boleyn. As her reign progressed, the persecutions largely came to an end. She was determined to rule for all her people. Catholics were informed that they would not be punished for their religion, only for actions harmful to the realm. The Church of England came into being during her reign. She did not like the Reformation zeal of the Scots such as John Knox, with their influence from Calvinist Geneva. Although the liturgy was again in English, she liked the ornate services, vestments and rituals of the Catholic services and did not want to see them go. The Book of Common Prayer of Edward was revised because it was too Protestant. She settled for a halfway house, an English compromise - hence the presence of both evangelicals and Anglo-Catholics in the Anglican Church today.

Elizabeth's tolerance, unusual for its time, was threatened by two developments. Her excommunication by Pope Pius V made it difficult for an English Catholic to be a loyal subject. The execution of Mary Queen of Scots angered Philip II of Spain who sent an armada consisting of 160 ships and 30,000 troops to take England for Rome. England seemed in desperate straits. She had no allies and the might of Europe was against her. Francis Drake led her to victory.

Two years after Elizabeth's death in 1603 came the Catholic attempt at treason which finally gave Protestant bigotry its chance. After the Gunpowder Plot of 1605 had been discovered, and King James I and parliament saved from death by explosion, November 5 was decreed an annual day of thanksgiving. This was named Guy Fawkes' Day after one of the conspirators. In a few places it remains, to this day, an opportunity for anti-Catholic propaganda as much as for fireworks.

The conflict in Northern Ireland between Protestants and Catholics is an outrageous anachronism - a religious war more in keeping with the 16th or 17th century. But its origins lie here and the reason was that politics and religion were inseparable. Church and State were still inexorably linked despite the creation of the Church of England. The Reformation did not go all the way back to the New Testament pattern of church life. It settled for a compromise between the old Roman Catholic traditions and the reforms proposed by the likes of Calvin or the Puritans.

Oliver Cromwell (1599-1658) was Lord Protector of England in 1653. He had a vision of a Puritan theocracy and did much to bring reforms to both State and Church. He refused the title of king, and ensured that England would be ruled by Parliament and not absolute kings. He reorganised the Church of England, trying to provide faithful preachers in every church. He protected Quakers and Jews alike. He was regarded as a man of vision, motivated not by personal ambitions but by his Christian faith.

15

PROTEST MOVEMENTS

AD 1600-1900

Puritanism

This was initially a movement within the English Church during the reign of Elizabeth I. Its general aim was to implement a full Calvinistic Reformation in England. The Bible as interpreted by the continental Reformers was held by Puritans to be the only source from which doctrine, liturgy, church structure and personal faith could be constructed. Bible reading in homes was encouraged, especially using the Geneva Bible. The preaching of the Word became the dominant aspect of the service, replacing liturgy. There was a strong emphasis on piety.

On their return from exile in Switzerland, many of these Protestants had great hopes for the Elizabethan church, but they were soon to be disappointed with the issuing of the Settlement of Religion (1559), since they felt that too many relics of Roman Catholicism were preserved. The Puritans and their parliamentary friends pressed for further reforms but Elizabeth would have none of this. After James I made it clear at the Hampton Court Conference of 1604 that he did not intend to make any important changes in the Church, the Puritans either compromised and remained within the Church of England or became "separatist".

Some of these went to Holland and others, such as the Pilgrim Fathers went to New England. After 1630, there was a large exodus of Puritans to Massachusetts, where they sought to create a purified Church. The Puritans in England, the "English Calvinists" with their vision of a Reformed nation and Church akin to the Geneva model, were largely unsuccessful in leading the way to Nonconformity in England. There were many notable preachers among the Puritans including Richard Baxter, Richard Sibbes and John Owen.

Baptists

The Baptist movement traces its roots back to John Smyth, one of the many English separatists in exile in Europe. In 1609, Smyth's English Separatist congregation in Amsterdam was led by a study of the New Testament to disband and reorganise itself, with believers' baptism as the basis of church fellowship. Smyth and most of his congregation applied to join the Mennonites, and were accepted by them in 1615, three years after Smyth's death.

Meanwhile, a small group under Thomas Helwys returned to England in 1612 and formed the first Baptist church on English soil in Spitalfields. They were the General (or Arminian) Baptists. The first Particular (or Calvinistic) Baptist church came into being around 1633. Both streams made great progress so that, by 1660, there were between 200 and 300 Baptist churches in England and Wales.

There were a number of notable Baptists at this time. John Bunyan (1628-1688) pastored a church of Baptists and paedobaptists. William Carey (1761-1834) spurred the ministers of the Northamptonshire Association to form the Baptist Missionary Society, persuading them to relax their rigid and extreme Calvinism. Carey himself went to India the following year, in 1793, marking the start of the modern missionary era. Charles Spurgeon (1834-1892) was widely influential as a preacher and a prolific writer.

Quakers

The founder of the Quakers, or Society of Friends, was George Fox

(1624-1691) from Leicestershire. He had no formal education but after a long and painful struggle came in 1646 to experience the "Inner Light of the Living Christ". He began preaching about the need for God to speak into the soul and would frequently disrupt church meetings that were not inspired and led by the Holy Spirit. One wonders what Fox would do today if he came into some of our meetings! In 1650 at Derby, he was imprisoned as a blasphemer and there a judge nicknamed the group "Quakers" because Fox had exhorted him to "tremble at the word of the Lord".

With their emphasis on the Spirit emerged the typical Quaker meeting where people waited in silence for the Spirit to speak in and through them. The "Inner Light" was as important as the Scriptures; sacraments, ceremonies and clergy were abandoned. Persecuted at home by Puritans and Anglicans alike, they evangelised North America. One of their leaders, William Penn, established the first colony in Pennsylvania. In 1796 they opened the first mental asylum in England, underlining their commitment to social reforms. Early in the 18th century, they began to oppose slavery and their efforts contributed to William Wilberforce's ultimate success. They opposed war, both on biblical grounds and on the conviction that warlike feelings are a sign that something is wrong with people's thinking and attitude to one another. Although refusing combatant duties, Quakers have a notable record of valiant ambulance service on and off the battlefield. To them also is due credit for our system of fixed price trading.

Pietism

It was not very long before further reforms were needed within the institutions of Lutheranism. Luther, as we had seen, did not go very far. Reformation of the Reformation was now needed. Pietism was the reform movement which developed within the Lutheran Church, protesting that it had become rigid in its confessions and liturgy but lacked life and godliness. The Pietists emphasised Bible reading, good works and holy life.

Leaders of the Pietist revival were Philip Spener (1635-1705) at Dresden and Francke at Leipzig University and later at Halle

University. They will best be remembered for their efforts to foster a desire for holy living, biblical scholarship, social concern and mission. The Pietists were also to have an influence on Count Zinzendorf's Moravian Church.

Moravians

Christian David (b.1690) was a wonderful character used in the founding of the Moravian movement. He was born into a devout Catholic family. Finding no peace, he wandered around Germany seeking for the truth. He finally met Pastor Schafer in Gorlitz, a Pietist, who showed him the way of salvation through faith. He returned to Moravia, preaching the gospel, but was met with opposition. Through his contact with Pastor Schafer, he met Count Zinzendof, also a Pietist, engaged in serving the Lord with Pastor Johann Rothe in Berthelsdorf, Saxony, near the Bohemian border. David told Zinzendorf about the needs of the believers in Moravia, and was invited by Zinzendorf to come and settle in his estates in Saxony. David returned to Moravia and brought a few families of believers, who settled about a mile from Zinzendorf's castle on a wooded hill called Hutberg, or Watch Mountain. This they renamed "Herrnhut", the Lord's Watch, and the first of the extensive buildings was started in 1722. The Moravian Church living as a community had begun.

The story goes that one day David left his tools while in the middle of building and walked the 200 miles to Kunwald in Moravia, where there were a number of believers, descendants of families that had belonged to the old church of the Bohemian Brothers, Unitas Fratrum. He brought back a party of these, among them the families of Nitschmann, Zeisberger and Toeltschig, afterwards to become well-known missionaries of the Moravian Church. As this place of refuge became known, many others joined from a variety of backgrounds - Moravian, German Pietists, followers of Schwenckfeld and other eccentric reformers. This inevitably led to tension in the community and divisions appeared until Zinzendorf intervened and brought order to the community. In 1724, Zinzendorf discovered a copy of the

Order of Discipline in the library of neighbouring Zittau. This was a document drawn up at the last meeting of the old Unitas Fratrum and was edited by Comenius. Zinzendorf then became aware of the historical roots of these new settlers on his estate and read the document to them. Such a spirit was stirred up among them that they resolved to restore the old Church, from which many members were descended. From this point on a revival was started. The Holy Spirit was poured out on the community so that the Moravian Church was turned into one of the most powerful praying and missionary movements in history.

Mission was a primary focus of the Moravians. The proportion of missionaries to home members was 1:60 compared with 1:5,000 in the rest of Protestantism during this period. As early as 1732, Nitschmann went to St Thomas, Virgin Islands; other work by the Moravians followed in Greenland (1733), North America (1734), Lapland and South America (1735), South Africa (1736), Labrador (1771), among the Australian aborigines (1850) and Tibet (1856). In England, following visits by Zinzendorf, Spangenberg and Toeltschig, a settlement was established along the Herrnhut model at Pudsey, between Leeds and Bradford. John Wesley owed his conversion largely to the Moravian, Peter Boehler.

Methodists

The nickname of "Methodist" was applied to members of the Wesleys' "Holy Club" at Oxford in 1729. This term, though rejected by Charles, was readily accepted by his older brother John, who supplied his own definition:

"A Methodist is one who lives according to the method laid down in the Bible."

John Wesley was the fifteenth child of the rector of Epworth in Lincolnshire, Samuel Wesley, and his wife Susanna. Although John's father was a High Churchman, both grandparents were Puritan Nonconformists. John was educated at Charterhouse and Christ Church, Oxford, and was ordained a priest in 1728, though he was still not truly converted.

Returning to Oxford, he found his younger brother, Charles, had gathered a few undergraduates, including George Whitfield, into a society for spiritual improvement. This Holy Club met for prayer, the study of the Greek New Testament, self-examination and charitable good works. Despite all the enthusiasm, John was troubled in his heart about his own salvation and inner peace.

In 1735, the Wesley brothers accepted an invitation from the Society for the Propagation of the Gospel to undertake a mission to the American Indians in Georgia. The project proved a fiasco and when he returned to England in 1738, John wrote: "I went to America to convert the Indians; but,oh, who shall convert me?" This was an expression of the emptiness he felt inside him despite all his theological training. On the journey to America, the Wesleys had met a group of 21 German Moravian missionaries whose simple faith had made a considerable impression on them, especially when they prayed during a storm. When, therefore, John was introduced in London to another Moravian, Peter Boehler, he was open to listening to Boehler's teachings in faltering English. This led Wesley to become "clearly convinced of unbelief, of the want of that faith whereby alone we are saved". On the back of a cart accompanying a prisoner on his way to be executed, Boehler exhorted Wesley to "preach faith until you have it, and then, because you have it, you will preach faith". The prisoner made a profession of faith and the change in him was so remarkable it clearly affected John. His father, on his deathbed had told John that he needed to have "the inner witness" of the Holy Spirit.

On May 24, 1738, John Wesley heard Luther's *Preface to Romans* read at a meeting in Aldersgate Street, London. He interrupted the meeting and testified that as he heard those words he "felt his heart strangely warmed". He became known as the "Apostle of the Burning Heart". Returning home to his room, he was flooded by the presence of God. This turned him into an evangelist and the Methodist revival had begun. "Then it pleased God to kindle a fire which I trust shall never be extinguished." Charles Wesley would take up this theme in his hymn "O Thou, who camest from above . . ."

Shortly after his conversion, John Wesley visited Count Zinzendorf in Herrnhut and was greatly helped by meeting him and witnessing at first hand the life of the Moravian Church community. On his return, he took up open-air preaching at the instigation of George Whitefield. It was at Kingswood, Bristol, that he took on "this strange way of preaching in the fields". This was because Wesley found himself rejected by the Church of England for his evangelical doctrines and evangelistic fervour. He wrote:

"Finding that the pulpits are denied me, and the poor colliers are ready to perish for lack of knowledge, I went to them, and preached on a mount to upwards of two hundred . . .I thought I might be doing the service of my Creator, who had a mountain for his pulpit, and the heavens for his sounding board . . . "

The next time he preached, 10,000 people came to hear him for one hour. He tells how

"the first discovery of their being affected was to see the white gutters made by their tears, which plentifully fell down their black cheeks as they came out of their coal-pits".

But this was to prove to be the most effective medium for reaching the masses and he was to give himself to the common people for the rest of his ministry. "The world is my parish", was his saying. Wesley drew crowds with his preaching, sometimes tens of thousands. It was accompanied by a power of the Spirit that nothing could resist.

Wesley organised his converts into classes and societies for discipleship and as a means of continuing evangelism. He travelled extensively between London, Bristol and Newcastle, the three points of a triangle. Wales was left to a colleague, Howel Harris. The districts were called "circuits" and Wesley would ride round each circuit once a month. In all, he travelled 250,000 miles on horseback in 50 years!

Wesley would preach the law until the congregation realised

their sin and need for God. Then he would preach the love of God. He actively trained and permitted laymen to preach locally. The Methodist revival in the 18th century affected Methodists, Baptists and the Church of England, resulting in the following:

- The churches were full of songs. The great hymn-writers of this period included Isaac Watts, William Cowper, John Newton, James Montgomery (son of a Moravian), and Charles Wesley.

- Social reforms were introduced including relief of the poor, prison reforms and the building of orphanages and schools. William Wilberforce campaigned against slavery.

- Missionary societies started at the end of the 18th century included the Baptist Missionary Society (1792), the London Missionary Society (1795), the General Methodist Missionary Society (1796) and the Church Missionary Society (1799).

These were the direct results of revival in the 18th century. It demonstrates that revival can and does change society with long lasting effects.

The Great Awakenings

There have been a number of revivals, spontaneous movements of the Spirit linked to the Anabaptists, Puritans and Pietists both in America and England. The Great Awakening began in 1720 when Theodore Frelinghuysen (1691-1747) came from European centres of pietism to pastor four Dutch Reformed churches in New Jersey. Under his influence, Gilbert Tennent, a Presbyterian, held revival meetings and started a school, dubbed the "Log College", which produced many revivalists. Tennent accompanied George Whitefield throughout the colonies in 1740-41 and was responsible for the founding of the College of New Jersey, better known now as Princeton University.

In 1734, revivals broke out in New England under the preaching of Jonathan Edwards, and by 1740 when Whitefield arrived bearing the spirit of the Wesleyan revival in England, the Awakening was widespread in America. Many were converted, resulting in controversies over extremism and causing splits in some of the denominations. The Second Great Awakening occurred mainly among middle-and upper-class Anglicans in England after 1790 and in America in colleges such as that at Yale University under Timothy Dwight in 1802, with great emotional and physical manifestations. Charles Finney's urban revival meetings of the 1830s have been considered to be a later flowering of the Second Great Awakening.

A lay interdenominational revival which developed through lunchtime prayer meetings in New York in 1857 led to more than half a million coming into the Church. A revival in 1863-4 brought 150,000 soldiers in the US Confederate Army into the Church. Similar awakenings happened in Britain and on the Continent. The mass evangelistic efforts in the 1870s of Dwight L. Moody and R.A. Torrey were estimated to have added 2.5 million to the Church. These revivals produced men such as Dr Thomas Barnado, the pioneer worker for children, William Booth, who founded the Salvation Army, and Hudson Taylor, the great missionary to China who founded the China Inland Mission (now known as Overseas Missionary Fellowship, OMF).

There was also the revival in Wales in 1904. This saw a great outpouring of the Spirit leading to conviction of sin and conversions. Since the early 1900s, there has been no revival in the industrialised West, but there have been revivals in Korea, East Africa, Indonesia and South America in the 20th century.

The Pentecostal Movement

One last significant movement needs to be mentioned to complete our story of the radical church. This is Pentecostalism which began as an outgrowth of the Holiness Movement in the United States of America. It had an evangelical faith with an added emphasis on the baptism of the Holy Spirit. While many of the truths had been recovered by this stage, it was left to this movement to restore to the Church its pentecostal dimension.

Recent scholarship has revealed some interesting insights into the beginnings of this movement. The first centre of Pentecostalism was in Kansas at the Bethel College founded in 1901 by Charles Parham. This was then moved to Houston, Texas, in 1905, where Parham taught that the "initial evidence" of receiving the baptism in the Holy Spirit was glossolalia, speaking in tongues. One of the students was the son of former slaves, William Seymour, who was to play a key role in this movement. Because he was black, he was not permitted to sit in with the rest of the class. He had to sit in the hall listening to Parham through the doorway! Parham shared many of the racist views of his time. He believed that mixing of races caused the flood in Noah's time and that Anglo-Saxons were descendants of the ten lost tribes of Israel.

After leaving Houston, Seymour brought the teaching to Los Angeles, where he founded the Apostolic Faith Gospel Mission in Azuza Street, in 1906. The revival that broke out was to spread throughout the world. Meetings were held in a tiny building packed with wooden benches three times a day, seven days a week for three years. Thousands came to receive this "baptism". Poor and uneducated people were very much at home in Azuza Street.

While glossolalia was the "new" manifestation and the one that has attracted most attention and emphasis, the remarkable unity of Seymour's Azuza Street revival was even more striking. Every nationality, race and culture attended the meetings. This unique mixing of blacks and whites under Seymour's leadership caused Frank Bartleman to comment : " The colour line has been washed away by the blood." Women's ministries were also encouraged. We said earlier that one of the manifestations of the coming of the Spirit was the tearing down of barriers. In the first century it was between Jews and Gentiles. Here it would be between blacks and whites. Racial prejudice miraculously disappeared when glossolalia appeared.

In contrast to Parham's authoritarian style, Seymour's leadership has been described as one of meekness. He would often sit with his head covered behind the rough shoe boxes used as the pulpit. His preaching was more that of a teacher and was not in the tradition of the black pulpit orator. He was a modest, unassuming man, blind in one eye but mighty in God.

When Parham visited Azuza Street, he was appalled to find "blacks and whites worshipping together, some shaking physically and others falling under the power". Parham's inability to cope with the racial mix and the exuberance of black worship led him to denounce this work. Parham left to set up a rival meeting in Los Angeles. Soon other whites who were originally with Seymour left to join Parham's white pentecostal movement. The rift between these two men was never healed. Where Parham had emphasised the individual experience of tongues, Seymour saw the power that was released in glossolalia worship working out corporately in tearing down the colour barrier. Thus was lost an opportunity for the creation of a new community of radical love cutting across all barriers.

Pentecostalism is undoubtedly the fastest growing movement in the world today. Practically every early Pentecostal movement in the world can be traced directly or indirectly to Seymour's Azuza Street. Through the Pentecostal Movement, the teachings about the Holy Spirit were passed on to the other mainstream churches so that today there is a broadly-based Charismatic movement with representatives from all the denominations. Perhaps all Pentecostal Churches and their offshoots in the Charismatic movement should examine themselves to see if their pentecostal experience embraces all races, cultures and classes, creating a new Spirit-energised community. Another aspect of the early Pentecostals' radical discipleship, which is not well known, involved their attitude to war. They were generally but not universally pacifists. They were influenced by the pacifism of the Holiness churches, as well as by leading evangelicals such as Alexander Campbell, of the Disciples of Christ, who was an absolute pacifist, and Moody, who was a conscientious objector in the Civil War. Parham married a Quaker, Frank Bartleman forbade Christians to go to war and in 1917, the Assemblies of God officially declared their opposition to war. In this also, they were therefore standing in the same traditions as the Anabaptists and other radical groups. The decline in pacifism among the Pentecostals basically corresponded to the trend in public opinion.

PART TWO

16

LESSONS FROM CHURCH HISTORY

Hindsight is the mother of all wisdom. With hindsight as our guide, we could all be wise. It is always easy to be critical of past failures in church history. Yet we must be so, humbly and soberly, because in them there is much that we need to learn and attempt to put right. No single group or individual was without its weaknesses. Those within the state-churches - Catholic or Protestants - were responsible for much bloodshed and aberrations by their alignment with the state authorities. However, some of those within the radical movements developed many weaknesses with successive generations - extremism, legalism, fanaticism and introversion.

We turn now to look at several issues that had a significant bearing on the story of the Church and we shall attempt to draw some lessons for today. There are many issues that one could choose, but this selection is based on the following criteria:

- Mistakes that have resulted in major distortions to the original church model.

- Emphases of the radical protest movements that have lessons for us today.

1. Church-State Relationships

No single issue has caused as serious a distortion to the nature of the Church as that of Church-State relationship. To understand the complexities of this issue, we need first to examine the nature of society. According to Verduin societies can be either composite or sacral.

A composite society is one composed of different factions and allows a diversity of opinions among its members. No one conviction or religion is forcibly imposed on all its members by the State. It is pluralistic. There is a freedom to exercise choice. An example of composition is democracy. Although Christianity has existed under totalitarian regimes, it is by nature composite in its view of the world:

"Authentic Christianity sees human society as composite, that is, consisting of people of diverse ways of thinking." (Verduin)

The Church was meant to be among other communities, a "society within society", peacefully coexisting alongside other socio-political groupings. It was never meant to forcibly "Christianise" the society.

A sacral society has a single religion which, it is assumed, embraces all its members. Religion is a matter of course, determined by birth into that society. There is to all intent and purpose, no real distinction between "Church" and "State". The offices of priest and king work hand-in-hand. Islam tends towards the sacral, with present-day Iranian society being the clearest example, where the priest (the Ayatollah) seeks to use the power of the state to impose Islam. Criticism of the State is regarded as criticism of Islam itself and vice-versa. Dissenters are regarded as both traitors and heretics.

However, we need not look at Islam and Iran for examples of sacralism. The tragedy is that for many centuries Christian sacralism was the norm in Europe. In Catholic Europe we have the twin cornerstone of Emperor and Pope ruling the Holy Roman Empire. Sadly the same was to be found among the Protestants. Luther in Wittenberg, Zwingli in Zurich and Calvin in Geneva all sought to impose their doctrines through an alliance with the civil authorities. It has been said of Calvin that

"he became the virtual ruler of Geneva till his death. His plan was to give the Church such authority that it could regulate the morals and religion of all citizens."
(Oxford Encyclopaedia)

For many, Geneva became a model city. In essence, the Reformation merely took "Catholic sacralism" and turned it into "Protestant sacralism", replacing Pope with Reformer. However honourable their intentions, the whole system was wrong from the start. Faced with the same option when the multitude wanted to make him king, Jesus withdrew from them, knowing full well that faith can never be enforced by civil authority but is a matter of personal conviction.

The first link between Christianity and State, between God and Caesar, began with the conversion of Constantine in AD 312. The Christians did not know what to expect from this conversion, which went beyond their fondest dreams. They were relieved when the Emperor suspended persecution; and many were glad when he began to accord financial benefits and other privileges to Christians. By the end of the fourth century, things had moved to the point where a later Emperor, Theodosius I, outlawed pagan worship and thus implemented the forcible "Christianisation" of the Roman Empire. These changes led to a system which has often been called "Constantinianism", which led to a drastic alteration of the entire landscape of Christian and European history, and which at times produced tragic and shameful consequences. When the union of Church and State took place, it produced a hybrid, hideous and un-Christlike, that would be responsible for the murder of tens of thousands.

The consequences of "Christian sacralism" were numerous. Among the most important were:

a) Coercion

Coercion is altogether reasonable in a sacral society. Anyone who does not conform must be forced to do so. In 392, Emperor Theodosius I made belief in Christianity a matter of imperial command. Participation in pagan worship became a crime liable to severe punishment. Christianity ceased to be voluntary, and was violently enforced. A biblical rationale for this had to be found. It was apparent to all that conversion by force was inconsistent for followers of Jesus, who had advocated enemy-loving. This theological rationale was supplied by Augustine of Hippo in an ingenious twisting of the Parable of the Banquet (see section on Biblical Hermeneutics). The consequence was disastrous. Refusing baptism, according to Charlemagne's book of laws, carried the death penalty. The chronicles tell us that on one day 4,500 reluctant Saxons were executed for not worshipping the right god. This behaviour would be repeated throughout medieval times. Along with conversion by coercion, violence was also used against heretics, Jews, dissenters and basically anyone within the monolithic sacral society who did not conform.

In 1524, many of the German peasants used Luther's teachings as a reason for revolting against serfdom. Luther hastily penned his tract Against the Murderous and Thieving *Hordes of Peasants*, which included the words:

"Let everyone who can smite, slay and stab, remembering that nothing can be more devilish than a rebel. It is just when one kills a mad dog."

The peasants were defeated and, in the usual pattern of events, the ruling classes of Protestant noblemen extracted a revenge far more brutal than the original offence. Some said that as many as 100,000 peasants were butchered in a frenzy of aristocratic reprisal. Luther's hasty words were never forgotten and, by many, never forgiven. It is tragic too that Zwingli, who in later years was increasingly occupied with political activities, should die fighting in the battle of Kappel to protect "Protestant sacralism" in Zurich from the Catholics; this in the face of the words of Jesus: "My kingdom is not of this world; otherwise My servants will take up sword and fight." The kingdom of God can never be protected or advanced by political alliances or military violence.

The bitter history of Northern Ireland has its origins here in

16th-century Europe and on a much larger scale. Catholics and Protestants were killing each other in order to impose their own brand of sacralism.

In a "Christian sacral" society, protest movements were regarded as a threat to public order and these dissenters were condemned as traitors and heretics. Despite much persecution, these radicals maintained that Christianity was by nature voluntary. The words of Peter Chelcicky, of the Unitas Fratrum, best capture this sentiment:

> "Coercion has no place in religion. Whoever is not sincerely brought to the Christian faith through preaching of the gospel will never be brought by force . . . "

The New Testament is in wholehearted agreement.

b) Toleration

Implicit in the discussion on coercion is that sacralism is always intolerant of diversity. There is no freedom of conscience. Only in the 17th and 18th centuries was there the beginning of toleration. This was due in part to the Enlightenment and the philosophical thinking of John Locke, who advocated the fundamental right of every person to liberty of conscience which the State had no right to remove. But fundamentally this was a Christian idea. Toleration really began with the strand of nonconformist Christianity we have been describing. The Anabaptists protested vigorously against persecution and spoke in favour of toleration. Chelcicky stated it and Hubmaier wrote a tract on it.

The American Constitution was the first to be formulated along these lines, resulting in the final separation of State and Church. This principle has always been one of the hallmarks of the protest movements. It is therefore not surprising that they too would contribute to the formulating of the First Amendment of the American Constitution. The unending persecutions in Europe resulted in many dissenters emigrating to the New World. They brought with them the belief in the freedom of conscience and the non-interference of the State in matters of conscience. These ideas were to lead Roger Williams in Rhode Island to start an experimental society built on the principles of entire liberty of conscience. More than anything else, the success of this pioneering society gave the precedent for the separation of Church and State provided by the First Amendment.

> "Here the Stepchildren of the Reformation (Verduin's name for the Anabaptists) have at long last lived to see their great hour in the history of the world" (Ernst Troeltsch).

We now live in a post-Constantinian era. With rare exceptions, Christianity has once again become a voluntary minority faith. Let us not forget our debt to those in the protest movements who preserved this aspect of our faith at such great human cost.

c) Nominal Membership

With Constantine's conversion, Christianity became for the first time a positive advantage in the furthering of careers. Special concessions were offered to Christians. Soon the rich were flocking into the Church for the sake of tax concessions or to avoid wearisome duties on city councils. If religion is a matter of some external ritual or mere birth into a society, it is not long before worldliness, moral laxity and low spirituality begin to characterise the Church. This was as true of the medieval Catholic church as it was of the Protestant state-churches.

d) Mission

Another outstanding feature of the sacral society is that there is no need for missions - either to those within the society (ad intra) or to those of another society *(ad extra)*. There was no mission ad intra because it is assumed that every member already shares a common religion. Anyone born into the State was automatically born into the official "state-church". Nor is there any need for mission ad extra.

> "A sacral society does not seek to infuse its religion into another society with which it comes in contact unless it has political annexation plans" (Verduin).

In that case, a representative of the civil power, accompanied by that of the ecclesiastical authority, invades the territory, colonises it and imposes its religion on its subjects. For example, in a typical Spanish conquest, a conquistador and a priest would both step ashore - the former to plant a flag of the civil authority of Spain, the latter to place a crucifix in the name of the religious authority. The cross and the sword went hand in hand in these annexations. It was the belief that the conquest was done in the name of God and for his benefit. For this reason, it was also assumed that God was on their side to "Christianise the primitive natives".

The spread of Protestant state-churches was carried out in a similar way. The strategy was to get the princes from the neighbouring cantons to adopt Protestantism - either militarily or through political diplomacy - and then impose "Protestant sacralism" on its subjects. This sort of activity, even though it has been called "mission", is nothing of the kind. Much of the spread of Protestantism in Germany was due to political expediency. The German princes who wanted to break from Rome's control were only too delighted to adopt Luther's new Protestant ideas as a means of gaining their independence. Luther's teachings and attack on the papacy served as a rallying point for the German aristocracy. Nationalism and self-interests were the major motives. They did not embrace the truth for its own sake, as is shown by their refusal to support too many reforms, especially those that would result in a loss of power over the masses. This was why they brutally quashed the Peasants' Revolt - peasants liberated by the gospel would begin to demand justice for the poor. This was considered too dangerous by the princes.

e). Baptism

The Early Church continued the practice of the apostles by preaching believers' baptism. As we have seen from the *Didache,* the quantity of water used was not important. First preference was for running water in streams and rivers. If these were not easily accessible, then bath water could be used. The *Didache* then allows for the "sprinkling of the head" in case of emergency.

The quantity of water was immaterial. What was at issue was that only those of a responsible age who had spent the time going through the catechisms, who could "renounce Satan" and join in the communion, were baptised. Baptism of children and then of infants was a development that took place from the late second century onwards. The first unambiguous reference to children's baptism is to be found in Tertullian's *On Baptism* and he was opposed to the practice. Tertullian (c.160-215) instructed the delay of baptism, especially in the case of small children, but there was no mention of infants. Hippolytus's *Apostolic Tradition* (ca.215) provided the first evidence that infant baptism was part of the custom of the Church and Cyprian the first clear theological exposition of infant baptism *(Epistle 58)* pre-Constantine.

As infant baptism became more widespread and since baptism was for the forgiveness of sins, the practice of infant baptism became a decisive argument for the doctrine of original sin. In the controversy against the Englishman Pelagius, Augustine of Hippo secured the triumph of the doctrine of original sin. One of his main arguments was from infant baptism, which had become such an established practice that Pelagius, who denied original sin, could not deny the appropriateness of baptising children. Infant baptism did not immediately become uniform practice, however. There are many instances where children in Christian homes in the fourth century were not baptised until they were adults including some of the great leaders such as Ambrose, Basil of Caesarea and Gregory of Nazianzus.

The Reformers such as Zwingli were convinced from Scriptures at the early stages that believers' baptism should be the normal practice of the Church. The fact that he and the other Protestant Reformers failed to carry through this reform owes much to their sacral view of society. Anyone born into a Protestant State was automatically a member of the Protestant Church. What was required was a ceremony that received the newborn into the state church and the ceremony of infant baptism suited this purpose. There was then a dual role for infant baptism as practised by the state churches from the fourth century to today. The first was the forgiveness of sins and the second, the receiving of the newborn as members of the State and Church.

Infant baptism was therefore seen to be integral to the state-church concept. The Reformers and their political masters were understandably reluctant for change here despite the teachings of Scripture. This was why, although baptism was not the initial issue of controversy between the Anabaptists and the Protestant Reformers, it became the symbol of the radical church view. Believers' baptism cuts across the state-church concept and returns the Church to its original concept as a voluntary gathering of believers. This explains, in part, why the Anabaptists were so mercilessly persecuted by the authorities. Re-baptism or adult baptism was regarded as both heresy against the Church and treason against the State.

Christian sacralism today

What about Christian sacralism today? In the United States of America, the rise of evangelical Christians into a powerful political force, known as the Moral Majority and the Christian New Right, has been a significant phenomenon. Within a period of six years, this movement became one of the most formidable forces in American politics with millions of registered members and millions of dollars to back "suitable" candidates with a moral agenda. The result is that all presidential hopefuls have to be "born again". The civil liberties movement has reacted with shock to these events, labelling Jerry Falwell as an Ayatollah and the Moral Majority as a Far Right Nazi movement. Norman Lear and the People of the American Way have set up to oppose the Moral Majority (now the Liberty Federation) and do not want any religious influence in the running of the State and the schools.

What is happening here is the age-old tension between Church and State. Both extremes - those who want to eliminate religion from political life, as well as those who want religion to dominate politics - have overreacted. We do need structures to create order and prevent chaos. The Church was not intended for this nor is it equipped. When it has tried this in the past, it has brought enormous grief and suffering to all. And yet the Church is called to be salt and light in the world. Total withdrawal from the world is not the answer. How do we salt our society? How should Church and State relate together? This is an ongoing issue where we need much wisdom from God and more light from his Word.

It is a touch ironic that some Christians in the United States, which gave the world the first model of a composite society, should now be talking about some kind of sacralism. In places such as South Korea, Nagaland (northeast India) and Singapore, where there has been rapid church growth, Christian political influence can now be felt. Christians in these countries will have to grapple with the same issues as the Church has done throughout its history. How are they going to relate to society? Can the Church wield political influence without being corrupted ultimately by the world? Jesus gave a warning that once salt has lost its saltiness, it is of no use whatsoever.

One of the best models we have from church history is that of the Wesleyan revival. This period saw the conversion of thousands in England resulting in moral, social and economic changes in society. It did not however have a "direct" role in government, seeking instead to salt the nation by preaching, living a new lifestyle and setting an example for the rest of society. Wilberforce had more of a direct influence as a parliamentarian but he acted as an individual, not as a representative of the Church.

Perhaps there may lie some lessons for us today from this period of history. But we also have the model of the New Testament and Early Church. Here were visible communities of believers living out radical jubilee life-styles and salting the societies of their day. They did not seek to influence society through political means. They understood that the kingdom they belonged to was heavenly and could not be established by earthly political means. For the first 300 years, Christians did not have access to political power and yet they changed the world during that time through their discipleship.

The temptation to take up political power for the good of the

Church and society will always be there. However, power corrupts and absolute power corrupts absolutely and there is nothing more abhorrent than a religious tyrant. The temptation to use political power for good cuts both ways. In an alliance of Church and State, the Christians may be granted influence that will change society for the good. Christian values and order may be imposed. All this is to be commended and welcomed. However, the problem arises when the State requires the Church to support policies and actions which the Church believes are immoral or unjust. During the Second World War, "Lutheran Germany" was placed in exactly such a predicament. Whilst Martin Niemoller and Dietrich Bonhoeffer opposed Nazism and the declaration of war, Hitler had the support of Bishop Ludwig Muller and the Lutheran Church. The religion of Nazism was blended with Lutheranism.

Sooner or later, the world will extract its price for such a partnership. In the temptation story, Satan offered Jesus the kingdoms of this world in return for his worship and allegiance. Jesus refused to sell his soul in order to gain temporal political power. His disciples will do well to follow His example. The Constantinian model of Church and State is still around. Do we need to pray for a disengagement of Church and State in the Anglican, Roman Catholic and Reformed Churches? Should the Queen remain the head of the Church of England or should we return to a biblical model of church government? This question is not asked out of disrespect for the Queen, for whom I have much admiration. She is a wonderful Head of State. But the state-church model is a hybrid produced by a quirk in history. Is it time for it to be dismantled? I believe that one of the effects of the Holy Spirit's visitation in these days is to restore the Church to its original foundations. Our churches today may welcome the Holy Spirit for the manifestations of spiritual gifts, but he will not stop there. Once inside the Church, he will have other "surprises" for us. He is committed to bringing renewal to all aspects of church life, not just the pentecostal dimension. He will challenge us about our doctrines, worship, discipleship, economic sharing and our organisation. Hold on to your seats, there are more earthquakes to come! He has come to get the Church ready for the Lord Jesus, and will not stop until that task is completed.

Christian sacralism in the future

We have argued strongly for a separation of Church and State on the basis of scripture and lessons from church history. And yet there will come a day when there will be a Christian sacral society on earth. This will take place in the millennium, when the Church will rule the world. It will only happen after the Lord returns, not before. There will be a "Christendom" after all! The problem with Constantine, Zwingli and Calvin was they wanted this Christendom before Jesus's Second Coming. We will all have to wait for the parousia to see the nature of this heavenly kingdom worked out on earth. This should be something to look forward to!

2. The role of the Bible

The Bible is the most "dangerous" book in the world. It contains the gospel, which is the power of God for salvation. It sets people free to live as God intended. It will change lives and change the world. Above all, it contains the revelation about Jesus. Men and women who encounter Jesus in the pages of the Bible have been transformed and challenged to imitate him by their radical discipleship. No wonder then that one of Satan's strategies has been to keep Christians away from reading the Bible. He has been remarkable successful. For centuries, ordinary Christians were kept from reading and studying the Bible. Those bold enough to meet privately for Bible studies were punished (sadly, this is still true in some countries today). The "authorised version" for centuries was the Vulgate Bible in Latin, read only by the professional clergy, who alone could understand the Scriptures. Even they could not interpret the Bible - the Pope alone could provide an infallible interpretation. With the language difficulties (only the educated learnt Latin), high illiteracy and its general inaccessibility, the Bible was a closed book to the masses for many centuries. The truths of God were locked within the pages of the Bible unread. The hungry children could not get access to the Bread of Life.

Lest we think that it was only the Catholic Church who was doing this, we should remember that the civil authorities of Zurich under Zwingli also banned independent Bible study groups because of the Anabaptist threat. There are still churches today who are afraid of these "unofficial" gatherings around the Word.

It is argued that before the advent of printing it would have been difficult to make the Bible generally available. There is some truth to this. However, looking at the protest movements, we see there a strong determination that every disciple should know God's Word. For them the supremacy of the Scriptures was predominant. The Waldensians and the Lollards memorised Scriptures, and it was not unusual for their lay people to memorise the entire New Testament and large sections of the Old Testament. If the established churches had felt its importance, they could have done the same. Their neglect was because of the fear that a study of Scriptures might have exposed their errors. It was easier to control and rule the masses when they were illiterate and ignorant of God's truths. For the ordinary people, the Bible was a magical book. Its words were viewed superstitiously and its truths could only be known by the elite class of enlightened and ordained clergy. Rejecting the medieval synthesis of Scripture, tradition and papal authority, the protest movements without exception have all consistently held the view of the Scriptures as the sole authoritative guide to faith. One of the principles rooted in church history is that renewal movements always begin with a study of the Scriptures. Again and again, the Word of God has been the trigger and inspiration for renewal and recovery of lost truths.

This is a very biblical pattern. The vision for the return of the nation of Israel from exile in Babylon was conceived as Daniel read from the scroll of Jeremiah. The reformation of Israel under Ezra was based on the recovery of the Law. The Reformation in the 16th century was launched as a result of a return to the Scriptures. The Renaissance had sparked an intense interest in the study of the Bible in the original languages in such places as Basle and Nurnberg. Luther's writings about faith, salvation and church grew out of this particularly active period of biblical studies. The fresh translations of the Bible by Erasmus based on Greek manuscripts were the most powerful means of bringing about the Reformation.

The Radical Reformation was also started by the Swiss Brethren as they met to study the Scriptures together. In the early days this was done with Zwingli. However, when he retracted his views on State/Church and baptism, the Anabaptists began meeting separately for Bible study. Manz translated parts of the Old Testament from the original Hebrew into the vernacular. Grebel did the same for the New Testament from the Greek. These men were conscious that the truth needs to be widely available to all. The Hutterites had an impressive system of education aimed at teaching the Scriptures. When most of Europe was still illiterate, they organised a compulsory school system to ensure that all their members would be literate. They believed that their movement depended on an educated people who could practise New Testament discipleship. This was a remarkable achievement for their day and in marked contrast to the attitude of the state-churches, who felt no such need. For them, their religion remained in the hands of the professional class of clergy while the layman's chief function was one of subservient obedience. For this purpose, ignorance served as well as, if not better than, knowledge.

Long before the Reformers and the Anabaptists, others also saw the vital importance of getting the Bible into the hands of ordinary people so that they could hear it speak for themselves. Tyndale (c.1494-36), as we have seen, was convinced. He vowed that

> "if God spared his life ere many years, he would cause the boys that drove the plough to know more of the Scriptures than the divines who kept it from them".

Despite being hounded all over Europe, he completed the first edition of his New Testament translation into English in 1525. Before that, Wycliffe (c1329-1384) and his associates had translated the Latin Vulgate Bible into English, believing that the Scriptures were the only authoritative guide to faith and practice.

Nothing is more dangerous to Satan than to allow ordinary people access to the Scriptures. The Bible teaches truth as well as exposes errors. It gives teachings about faith as well as warnings against disobedience. Many truths lost from the Church for centuries have been recovered as men and women have gone back to the Bible. A selection of these and the groups who have restored biblical truth to the Church are listed:

GROUP	LESSON	BIBLE REF
Waldensians Franciscans	simple lifestyle evangelism	Matthew 5
Brethren of the Common Life	The inner life	Ephesians 5
'Early' Martin Luther	'sola fide'	Romans 5
Moravians Hutterites	Community Prayer for mission	Acts 4
Quakers Pentecostals	Tongues, prophecy	Acts 2
Anabaptists	Believers' baptism Pacifism	Acts
Pietists Puritans	Election Personal study	Ephesians 1
Methodists	Being born again outdoor missions	John 3
Salvation Army	Social concern Power of music	Acts 6

As John Robinson (c.1575-1625), the pastor of the Pilgrim Fathers, had prophesied: "There is yet more light to come from God's Word." How right he was.

The Bible in today's Church

1) Jesus had repudiated the Scribes and Pharisees for putting their oral traditions above that of the written Law. In keeping with this, the Early Church had started out with the Bible as the authoritative basis of faith and practice. From Constantine to the Reformation, Scripture was placed ostensibly alongside ecclesiastical traditions but in practice often below traditions. The Reformation restored the principle of *sola scriptura*, the Scripture as the sole authority. In practice, as we have seen, the Reformers were still very much guided by past traditions. It was left to the radicals to restore both the principle and the practice of *sola scriptura*. This is a return to the New Testament and we should guard against any tendency for " Scripture plus . . . ", whatever that something else may be. There is a tendency among certain sections of the Church today to place prophecy or rhema words, or experience, on a par with Scripture. We should resist this in view of the high price that has been paid to restore the authority of the Bible.

2) There are still many ecclesiastical and denominational traditions in our church life. Traditions can be helpful so long as they are not unbiblical. The only way the unbiblical traditions can be removed is through a committed return to the view of placing Scriptures above tradition.

3) In the medieval Church, the altar and the sacraments dominated the services. Later on, more liturgy in the form of music and set prayers was introduced. There was little room for the reading of Scriptures and even less for the preaching of the Word. All this was changed with the Reformers, Pietists, Puritans, Baptists and Wesleyans. Among them, as it always has been among the protest movements, the services were dominated by the pulpit, where the preaching of the Word was central. Up until recent years, the preaching of the Word had constituted the main part of the service in the evangelical churches. Recently however, among the charismatic churches, the trend has been to let charismatic praise dominate the services. Preaching time has been squeezed with

even less time for intercessory prayer. This cannot be healthy.

4) Throughout Church history, ordinary Christians were hindered from reading the Bible because of their illiteracy, the "sacredness" of the Latin language, and the rules of the Church. The hindrances today to the studying and preaching of God's Word are slightly different but no less real. One of the reasons is an underemphasis on the mind coupled with an overemphasis on the Spirit. There is an unhealthy anti-intellectualism among some charismatic churches today. We are not talking about the kind of intellectualism which is arid and arrogant. May God spare us that! However, in some of our churches anything which is mildly cerebral is thrown out. But our minds matter and they need feeding! We are instructed to love God with our minds as well as our hearts and to gird up our minds ready for action (1 Peter 1:13). Expository preaching is being substituted with experiential preaching and content replaced with comfort. We need to restore a balance of Word and Spirit. Someone has rightly said :

"If we emphasise the Word only, we dry up. If we emphasise the Spirit only we blow up. But if we have both, we will grow up."

This balance of Word and Spirit was a strong Anabaptist emphasis. There is an assault on our minds on a scale without parallel in history, be it in the form of pantheism, Monism, New Ageism or other "isms". Christians have to use their minds as well as their hearts to win people for the gospel. Within the Church, the influence of Naturalism/evolutionism is being felt even in our evangelical Bible colleges. This philosophical battle is as real today as it was in the New Testament and Early Church. We need to fight the battles on this front as surely as they did.

As we look at the structures, beliefs and practices of the Protestant churches today, it would appear that we are still more influenced by the teachings of the Reformers than by the Bible itself. There needs to be fresh hunger for God's Word in our generation. Only as we return to biblical faithfulness will we become the kind of Church that will again effect change in our society.

3. Mission

One of the paradoxes of Protestantism during the Reformation era is that while the Church was called back to its apostolic faith, the fulfilment of the apostolic mission was largely left to the Catholics and the radicals. On the subject of mission, Anglican historian Stephen Neill concluded:

"When everything favourable has been said that can be said, and when all possible evidences from the writings of the Reformers have been collected, it all amounts to exceedingly little."

A terrible indictment indeed, but one which is nevertheless true when the mission efforts of the Reformers are matched against the worldwide labours of Jesuits, Franciscans, Moravians and Wesleyans. Roman Catholic controversialists such as Bellarmine used to argue that the absence of mission among the Reformers proved that Protestantism was heretical. During the 17th century, one-third of all Roman Catholic missionaries died before reaching their mission field through shipwreck or disease.

Four major factors were responsible for this lack of mission in Protestant state-churches:

a) The Territorial church concept

We touched on this point in the section on Church/State issues. "As the prince, so the religion" (cuius regio eius religio) was the solution of the Peace of Westphalia to stop the bloody battles waged between Protestant and Catholic princes. Mission was unnecessary because every citizen was either born a Protestant or Catholic depending on the territory of his birth. The refusal by the Reformers to accept that the Church can only be a voluntary association of believers was a major hindrance to mission.

b) Predestination theology

The second major theological obstacle to mission was an extreme brand of predestination. The heathens were considered to have forfeited their right to receive the gospel because of their barbarity. "The holy things of God are not to be cast before such as dogs and swine" announced the Czech Calvinist, Ursinus. Furthermore if God wanted the heathen to be converted, he would see to it himself. It follows also that those born outside the boundaries of Europe, namely the Turks and other Muslims, were predestined for damnation, hence there was no need to evangelise them. This explains why for centuries within Protestant Europe there was no evangelism directed at the Muslim world. This absence of mission becomes even more poignant when one recalls how the spirit of Francis of Assisi burned for the conversion of the Muslims. Twice he almost suffered death in his efforts to preach to those in Palestine and Morocco. His efforts were rewarded when he was granted a personal audience with the Sultan and preached Christ to him.

c) Cessational theology

The Great Commission of Matthew 28 was explained by the Reformers to have been literally carried out by the apostles going to "all nations" and had therefore been fulfilled. Ingenious erudition was employed to demonstrate this, including a picture of three heads found in China as evidence of knowledge of the Trinity. Justus Menius, a 16th-century Lutheran theologian, argued that "God sent only the apostles into all the world"; all others were to follow the parish territorial system. This is hermeneutics tainted with cessationalism. Readers will recall that this kind of cessational argument was also used to explain the disappearance of spiritual gifts from the established churches.

d) Clericalism

The view of the Reformers was that preaching should only be carried out by state-ordained pastors, not by the laity. This view was backed by threats of punishment, as is shown by Luther's statement:

"Therefore let everyone ponder this, that if he wants to preach or teach let him exhibit the call or commission that drives him to it or else let him keep his mouth shut. If he refuses this, then let the magistrate consign the scum into the hands of his proper master - whose name is Meister Hans [that is, the hangman]".

These ideas were still very much alive two centuries later as evidenced by the advice given to a certain young man by Dr John Rylands, a respected leader of the British Baptists:

"Sit here young man. When it pleaseth the Lord to convert the heathen, he will do it without your help or mine."

The young man's name was William Carey, whose enthusiasm was not quashed by his encounter with Dr Rylands and other Baptist ministers of the day. Carey went on to publish his tract entitled *Enquiry into the obligations of Christians to use means for the conversion of the heathen* to prove his point. This publication has been described as the single most influential missionary treatise in the English language. In it, Carey disputed the prevalent teaching that the Great Commission was directed only at the apostles by quoting the explorations of Cook and others as evidence that there were portions of the globe completely unknown during biblical times. He challenged the predestination and dispensational theologies popular then.

Carey has rightly been hailed as the Father of Protestant Mission. But when one looks at the radical movements, we find that mission has always been one of their hallmarks. The Waldensians were such prolific evangelists that, in 1245, Pope Innocent IV complained that their heresy had spread so widely that it included princes as well as simple peasants. It was estimated that in the early 15th century,

"one-third of Christendom, if not more, had attended illicit Waldensian conferences. They have been called the first missionaries to disseminate a considerable knowledge of the Bible among the people.."(Henry Lea).

Franklin Littell has documented the thesis that the Anabaptists were the first to make the Great Commission the responsibility of every church member. Certainly the rapid spread of the movement is impressive evidence of this. The Hutterite missionary effort was a costly enterprise. It is estimated that 80 per cent of the missionaries died a martyr's death. Carefully planned and administered and persistent, the Hutterite programme sent missionaries across Europe from what has been called "perhaps the greatest missionary centre of the 16th century" (Robert Friedman).

In the 18th century, the greatest missionary movement was to be found among the Moravians. The Renewed Moravian Church was a fusion of the older strain of the Unitas Fratrum with the dynamic revival spirit of Pietism under Count Zinzendorf. In addition to their fame as a community where economic sharing was practised, the Moravian church had a strong emphasis on corporate prayer. The famous round-the-clock prayer watch in which Moravians prayed for the revival of the church for 100 years was the springboard for the evangelistic missions from Moravia. One in five members were involved in missions somewhere in the world. Missions were started among the American Indians and the Eskimos among other peoples. The vitality of this movement was quite amazing. Among the converts of the Moravian missions was John Wesley who himself brought many to Christ through the Methodist movement. There was, all in all, an incredible mission effort among these and other protest groups.

4. Discipleship

Among the protest movements, we consistently find a special emphasis placed on the Sermon on the Mount. To them it represented the "gospel at its sharpest . ..and in its clearest, most comprehensive form". It contains the spirit of the gospel and embodies more than a Utopian dream. Its lucid teaching represents the bedrock that should shape and form kingdom attitudes and behaviour.

We find this emphasis among the Waldenses, the Anabaptists, the Unitas Fratrum, the Hutterites and also Francis of Assisi and Thomas à Kempis. In their "imitation of Christ", the Sermon has been a continuous source of inspiration. To them, love was the pre-eminent characteristic of the disciple. Gentleness, purity of heart, mercy, lovers and makers of peace - these were the ingredients

195

of love. Among such we consistently encounter a gentleness of spirit, a graciousness of words, a simplicity of lifestyle and an integrity of character that befits kingdom citizens.

Their understanding of the Sermon led many within the protest movements to a position of non-resistant pacifism. Two strands of thought led them to this position. The first is that loving God is intricately linked to loving people; that one cannot hate, kill, persecute or mistreat God's image without it reflecting on our love of God. Second, they saw that one of the most radical of the new ethics introduced by Jesus, indeed possibly the most radical, the loving of one's enemies, was to be obeyed and not bypassed or explained away as either irrelevant or unrealistic. From Augustine to Luther to 20th century evangelicalism, the enemies referred to by Jesus in Matt. 5:43 and Luke 6:27-36 have been interpreted to mean "personal enemies". Convenient as that might be, it would seem very clear from the context that it is Israel's national enemies, the Romans, who are referred to here. Not all the protest movements were pacifists. Even among the Anabaptists, there was a divergence of views on this issue. While the majority were indeed pacifists, there were those such as Hubmaier and the church at Nikolsburg who adopted the "Just War" position, maintaining that defensive wars were permissible. They were called Schwertler (men of the sword) by the pacifists. This should not obscure the fact that repeatedly, among the Franciscans, Waldensians, Lollards, Quakers and early Pentecostals, the renewal movements have seen a return to the pacifism of the Early Church as part and parcel of the cause of renewal.

We need to grapple with this important issue of peace. Clearly, there is a place for individual Christians to be involved in society - including maintaining law and order. There has to be a use of force to restrain the criminal and subversive elements within society. Christians living in countries colonised and occupied by a foreign power are instructed to love their enemies. This was the political context of Jesus' teaching in the Sermon on the Mount. Israel was a nation occupied by Roman enemies. However, we have no clear teachings about whether Christians can participate in offensive or defensive wars. This was why in the Early Church there were those who were absolute pacifists and those who allowed Christians to join the army, on condition that they did not kill. Two additional comments, however, are appropriate. First, there is a tendency throughout Church history for Christians to explain away the harder sayings of Jesus, such as "Pray for those who persecute you", "Go sell all your possessions and give to the poor", "Lend without expecting anything in return" and many others. The reason for such avoidance is surely that such commands point us to the cross and people have tended to shun paying such a high personal cost. This is what Bonhoeffer referred to as "cheap grace" - discipleship without the cross.

Second, it is interesting to note within the renewals of the 20th century, a movement towards recovering and facing up to many such hard sayings with one exception: that of loving one's enemies. This is still not a sufficiently "spiritual" issue to be discussed among renewal groups. However, it is the only issue where Jesus teaches that we shall be most like our Father: "You shall be called sons of God". We shall be most like our Father in reflecting his character when we are all-embracing and indiscriminate in the way we love, and that includes both personal and national enemies. The practice of this aspect of discipleship by the early Christians and the protest movements was revolutionary.

Historically church movements have squabbled over the details of orthodox belief statements, but rarely have they given us concrete examples of what the Christian ethic of love might actually look like in action. We catch a glimpse of this, however, when we observe the protest groups in their imitation of Christ.

5. The mark of suffering

According to Luther, a positive sign that God is present in the Christian is the experience of suffering. God and the world are enemies. The world will call those who serve God "fools". Those who hold to the Truth will be persecuted and will suffer. Jesus himself gave us a warning that "if they persecute me, they will also persecute you . .." (John15:20).

If this is true, it is quite clear as one contemplates the history of the Church that it is the "dissenters" who have suffered most under the Inquisition, at the stake and from state-church instigated crusades. The Church, like her Lord, has been called to serve as a suffering servant in this world. This service involves suffering, but never the inflicting of suffering on others. Sadly, the Church has often been responsible for much of the bloodshed.

"The Inquisition alone is enough to justify the claim that Christianity is the most cruel and barbarous of religions." (Jean Plaidy)

Is this not a tragic indictment of the followers of the only religious leader who has ever taught that we should love one another as well as our enemies, both national and personal?

During the first three centuries, the status of Christianity as religio illicita brought upon the early converts ten major persecutions, during which time thousands were martyred. The persecutions ended when Constantine embraced Christianity and made it the official religion of the Empire. By 392, belief in Christianity was made a matter of imperial law, punishable by death. Within a few years, the Church had changed from being the persecuted to being the persecutor, and paganism, heresy, Judaism and dissenters were violently suppressed. This marked the beginning of the long history of bloodshed which was to include the Inquisition, the Crusades, the Peasant Wars - all done in the name of Christ.

Many of the protest groups were subjected to severe persecution because of their radical nonconformity. Over a period of 11 days in June 1569, the Waldensian population of the Calabrian area of Italy was eradicated by Catholic troops from Spain. Some 2,000 were executed and 1,600 imprisoned. Concerning the Anabaptists it has been said that:

"A larger proportion of Anabaptists were martyred for their faith than any other Christian group in history - including even the early

Christians on whom they modelled themselves." (Gascoigne)

During the 16th century, by an alliance with the State, three Protestant groups won for themselves the position of established churches in different parts of Europe: the Lutherans, the Calvinists and the Anglicans. From the start, the Anabaptists were the outsiders, the radical wing of the Reformation, persecuted by Catholics and Protestants alike. For them, as for other Protestant minority groups - the Huguenots in France and later the Nonconformists in England - the 16th and 17th centuries represented one long and frequently bloodstained search for tolerance and freedom of conscience. Manz was the first Protestant to die at the hands of a Protestant government although others before him had been killed by Catholic authorities. Drowning became a common way of execution for the Anabaptists - a mordant play on the practice of adult baptism.

The history of the Church has been stained with much blood. These believers participated in "completing the sufferings of Christ". We can be certain that wherever the blood of God's people has been, and is still being spilt, whether it be in China, Uganda, Vietnam or medieval Europe, there God is building his Church. Perhaps this is why churches in the persecuted developing countries are experiencing such remarkable growth today.

6. Abuses of the Bible

To trace the history of biblical interpretation, or hermeneutics, would span many volumes and would require someone much more competent than me. However, one particular aspect is of relevance to our discussion, and it is that throughout church history there have been numerous incidences of the misuse and abuse of the Bible. Some have been relatively harmless and in fact rather amusing, the product of wild sanctified imaginations. Others are of a more serious nature and have led to major distortions in the nature of the Church.

There have been two major tendencies of biblical abuse. The first, as already mentioned, is to explain away the hard sayings of Jesus and the New Testament writers. There has been a tendency to spiritualise and attach mystical interpretations to them, a tendency that is very much alive today. However, in the 20th century, more sophisticated tools are used to explain away the uncomfortable passages. We now "demythologise" and subject passages to "higher criticism" or simply interpret them within the context of non-biblical presuppositions and world views. Biblical scholarship, which is sorely needed today, is not to be decried but must be carried out within the framework of biblical presuppositions. If the liberal theologians indulge in "demythologising", the charismatics and evangelicals have a tendency of "spiritualising" away the hard sayings of Jesus about carrying the Cross, enemy-loving, cancellation of debts, giving without expecting anything in return.

The second tendency has been to use Scriptures to justify certain actions or practices by the Church, including ecclesiastical buildings, vestments, the priesthood, the papacy, the Crusades - the list is endless. This has been achieved by a variety of methods. Sometimes it was pure syncretism - a synthesis of Christianity with Greek and pagan philosophy and practices. Some of the teachings today on "inner healing and wholeness" are a blend of popular "selfism" psychology (see Dr Paul Vitz's *Psychology as Religion*) and Christianity. Much of inner healing and counselling is an introspective pampering to "self". There are teachings today on "faith" praying and spiritual warfare that are rooted in eastern mysticism and the occult, including teachings about visualisation. These are syncretist tendencies that have to be tested against Scriptures. At other times, Christians have been involved in a wrong use of the Scriptures especially the Old Testament. Much of the justifications for war, apartheid and genocide have been based on the failure to understand that the Old Testament is not a static but a dynamic development in revelation; that what is foreshadowed in the Old Testament is fully revealed and fulfilled in Jesus, who is God's final word on any issue. Others have engaged in blatant twisting of Scripture. The biblical "justification" for the lack of mission by state-church Protestantism has already been discussed. Even more tragic was the biblical "justification" for conversion by coercion. This teaching has been responsible for the murder of hundreds of thousands throughout church history and represents the most tragic example of perverting Scripture.

The man responsible was Augustine of Hippo who explained that it was right and proper, indeed a sacred duty, to coerce and enforce conversion because Jesus said in the parable of the banquet:

"Go out into the highways and byways and compel them to come in, that my house may be filled." (Luke 14:23)

In their bloody campaigns, Catholic and Protestant authorities alike have either quoted Augustine directly, or else have been influenced by this interpretation. This distortion of biblical truth has been one of the factors responsible for the Catholic-instigated Inquisition, the Crusades and the joint persecution of the radical protest movements by Protestants and Catholics.

A corollary to the "doctrine of coercion" is what has been described as Christianity's least attractive feature, that is its long tradition of anti-Semitism. Matthew records that the Jewish crowd clamoured for the death of Jesus with the words: "His blood be on us and on our children" - a statement used to justify the belief that the Jews lay under the total and final curse of God. The First Crusade was launched with a massacre of thousands of Jews, particularly in German towns. Such an anti-Semitic purge was to become a traditional feature at the start of all the Crusades. In the 14th century, Europe experienced its most disastrous plague - the Black Death - which prompted many hysterical responses, including the traditional one of anti-Semitism. Word was spread that the Jews had caused the plague. More Jews were killed in reprisal for the Black Death than in any persecution up to the 20th century. Only in 1974 did the Vatican at last announce that the Jewish people were no longer to be held responsible for the crucifixion. In 1993, the Vatican finally recognised the State of Israel.

The popularity of anti-Semitism meant that many key figures

in Church history have been involved, including the likes of Ambrose of Milan, John Chrysostom, Erasmus and Martin Luther. When a Jewish synagogue was burnt in Rome in 388, restitution was enforced by Emperor Theodosius. The same would have happened in Callinicum if Ambrose had not insisted, unreasonably and to his lasting discredit, that it was sinful for a Christian Emperor to help the Jews to triumph over the Church. The anti-Jewish discourse of the otherwise brilliant expositor, John Chrysostom, were likewise particularly distasteful. Even the great humanist of the 16th century, Erasmus succumbed to the error of anti-Semitism as is shown by his statement:

"If it is incumbent upon a good Christian to detest the Jews, then we are good Christians."

Luther himself, despite his early sympathetic pamphlet Jesus was born a *Jew*, reversed his position in later years and lashed out with brutal vehemence at the Jews in a series of blatantly anti-Semitic pamphlets. In *Concerning the Jews and their Lies*, he advised his followers to eradicate Jewish homes and synagogues by burning them to the ground and covering the site with dirt; prayer books and copies of the Talmud were to be seized and destroyed; young Jews were to be enslaved at hard tasks. As a final step, Luther advocated expulsion:

"Let us drive them out of the country for all times . . .so that we may all be free of this insufferable devilish burden - the Jews."

This is a far cry from the apostolic faith of the New Testament and represents a major aberration in the history of the Church. How strange that Christians should love the God of the Jews but hate the Jews with such intensity. What repentance is required by the Church today towards the Jews.

It was not only in his attitude to the Jews that Luther reversed his stance to accommodate a worldly view. It can be seen in many of his other doctrinal positions regarding the Church, separation of Church and State, and baptism. This has prompted scholars to distinguish between "early" and "late" Luther. Furthermore,

Luther's anti-semitic writings have a chilling prophetic ring about them. In Nazi Germany, anti-Semitism reared its ugly head again and the systematic annihilation of six million Jews was carried out. This time there were Christian protest movements, that led by Dietrich Bonhoeffer perhaps the best known. Tragically, the land that gave rise to the Reformation through a return to the Scriptures was also the scene of the most horrific Holocaust.

Before we become overly smug about the failures of the past, perhaps we should heed that in the present day, Scriptures are being used to justify forms of liberation movements, wars, racism, tithing and theology of prosperity among other things. Unless we treat Scripture with reverence and study it in its historical-grammatical context, within the biblical environment and interpret Scripture with Scripture, we too may be led down the slippery theological slopes. Supremely we should have a Christological approach to Scripture and test all our interpretations against the character of the Jesus revealed in the gospels. The Anabaptists and many of the protest groups followed Jesus in adopting this approach to their understanding of Scriptures (Luke 24:27,44ff)

7. The Dialectic Process

There is some truth in the Hegelian dialectic which states that truth is arrived at by thesis and antithesis to produce a synthesis. We swing between extremes of views before arriving at some new point. The only difference with Hegel is that we believe there is an absolute truth which is not a proposition but a person, Jesus Christ, as revealed in the Bible.

Throughout history, the Church has demonstrated a knee-jerk reaction to numerous issues and in the process found itself over-reacting. To change metaphors, babies have been thrown out with the bath water. The Montanist extremism caused the established Church to react against the work and gifts of the Spirit. As a result, the supernatural gifts of the Spirit were largely lost and teachings arose to justify their cessation. It is the nature of people to react. The correct response to wrong use is not non-use but right use of the gifts. We should resist the temptation to react to excesses by swinging to the other extreme. Instead, our approach should be a return to Scriptures to discover the truth, which is often somewhere in the middle ground. And on issues where we cannot be absolutely certain, history should teach us to be more gracious and humble about the views that we hold because even the most able theologians, such as Augustine, Luther and Calvin have been proven wrong. Sincerity about our beliefs is not enough because we can be sincerely wrong. It is certain that this aspect of history will repeat itself many times over.

There are many issues being debated today that demonstrate these over-reactions. The Church has swung from rigid liturgical services to totally unstructured charismatic ones; we have gone from all hymns to all choruses, from set prayers to exclusively extempore prayers. We have reacted against the "social gospel" of the liberals and thrown out the call to social holiness. These are reactions which need balancing. Feminism is also one of these issues undergoing some dialectic process. The Church has neglected the place of women despite the radical actions Jesus took to restore womanhood to its rightful place. There has, however, been an over-reaction to this neglect and some Christians have followed the world's lead in all feminist matters. The extreme forms of Calvinism and Arminianism are other examples of this dialectic process. Both positions contain truths, but taken to extreme, both are erroneous.

We should learn from Church history that no one person or group has a monopoly on truth. They all had some "quirks" in their theology. Let us therefore learn from the past and seek to walk humbly with God and with each other.

17

HOW RADICAL ARE WE?

We started out with a survey of the nature of the Early Church and described it under the five headings : evangelical, pentecostal, sacramental, radical and organisational. We will conclude by examining the Church in the Twentieth Century to see where we now stand on these issues. To do this will involve some generalisations, not least because all the churches and radical groups - then and now - were not homogeneous in their creed and conduct. Accepting these limitations, it will nevertheless prove useful for us to summarize this study with some self-reflection. We need to hear what the past has to say to the present.

1. Evangelical
a) Salvation

The Early Church's evangelical doctrines on salvation gave way during the Catholic era to a sacramental view. Instead of salvation by grace through faith in Christ, the Catholic Church advocated sacerdotalism, salvation through the Church and its sacraments. Later on, abuses such as penance, indulgences, Mariolatry and simony crept in and were tolerated. The Reformation restored the teaching of justification by faith and rejected salvation by works. It was *sola fide* and *sola gratia* for the Lutheran Church. However, in his rejection of salvation by works, Luther over-reacted and undervalued the importance of the "good works that God had prepared before hand that we should walk in them"(Eph 2:10).

When Christians are taught that it is only grace and faith that matter and that obedience to Christ is secondary for their salvation, moral laxity is inevitably the result. Grace without obedience and discipline leads to licence. So vehement was Luther against any kind of works that he felt the Epistle of James, the "epistle of straw" as he called it, should not have been part of the canon of the New Testament. Among the radical groups, faith and works have always been held together. We may be saved by faith but we shall be judged by our works. The mainline Protestant Churches today need to maintain the Biblical balance to avoid the excesses of the past

b) The Bible

The high view of Scripture and the practice of regular Bible study and teachings among the early Christians was replaced by a magical and elitist approach during the Catholic period. The Bible stood alongside ecclesiastical traditions and often was subordinate in authority. Only trained and ordained clergy could study the Word. The Christians, "the People of the Book", were being kept from the Book. The Reformation's most significant contribution was to make the Bible an open book again for Christians. What a debt we owe to Wycliffe, Tyndale, Erasmus, Luther and countless others - not to forget the inventors of the printing press! As we have argued, although in principle the authority of the Bible was restored among the Reformed churches, in practice ecclesiastical traditions and political necessity still had a major role in determining, creed as well as conduct. Luther, because of political expediency, hung on to much of Catholic tradition although Calvin went further with his reforms. But these halfhearted changes were never satisfactory. The Pietist movement arose as a result of a desire to return to a New Testament experience, if not always a New Testament view of the Church. It seems that when the Church deviates from the Scriptures, God sets in train a process of recovery which does not stop until the Church has been called back to its roots in faithfulness to the Scriptures. Others, such as Luther, may stop once some truths have been recovered, but not God. God has an agenda to bring the Church to maturity and this can only happen when we embrace his whole counsel.

In the 20th century, there has been a fresh assault on the authority of the Bible - this time through the schools of liberal theology emanating from Germany. Sadly, the land that gave us the Reformation and brought us back to the Bible was also responsible for calling into question the authenticity of the Bible. The challenge for the Reformed and Lutheran Churches is to encourage evangelical scholarship in their seminaries. This is not to say that there is nothing of value in the Liberal theologians; on the contrary, I have found that their challenges to the Evangelical school serve as a useful foil. We need to establish clearly, however, that theism rather than rationalism or evolutionism is the right worldview for understanding the Bible.

There is also a threat today from the more charismatic sector of the Church to place prophecy, vision and experience alongside Scripture. There is a tendency amongst such to interpret Scripture by their experience instead of testing their experience with Scripture. This is a repetition of "late" Montanism. Is this high view of Scripture going to be lost again through such practices? Prophecies are imperfect because our knowledge is partial (1Cor. 12:8f). Will the place of the Scriptures be supplanted and replaced by other things? Church history has shown that those who teach or practise "The Bible plus .. . " will be preyed upon by unbelievers or their own leaders.

Of course, all charismatic leaders want to be regarded as conservative evangelicals in their doctrines. The tele-evangelists who have expounded unbiblical views have found their financial support threatened and a few have recanted. However, what they claim to profess is often very different to what they practise. In reality, the manifestation of the charismatic gifts is now a more important component of their services than the preaching of the Scriptures. If the Bible is used at all, it is to endorse their distinctive beliefs and practices. There is an emerging "charismatic hermeneutics" which seems to be largely self-centred, emphasizing the emotional and existential, paying no regard to the historical context. But God is not mocked: if we sow in the teachings of the gurus of 'positive confession' or 'selfism', the harvest we will reap will ultimately be disastrous for the Church.

c) Evangelism

The Early Churches' evangelistic zeal evaporated in the centuries after the Constantinian change. There was no need for evangelism if Christianity was the *religio licita* and all others *religio illicita*. The number and quality of disciples grew despite, and maybe because of, persecution. With the exception of the missionary activity growing out of the Catholic Reformation, this period of non-mission extended through the Middle Ages and Reformation era until the 19th century, when the great missionary movements started in the established churches. The protest movements have, however, always been evangelistic. They did not subscribe to the territoral church concept and saw the Great Commission as a mandate for the whole Church and not just to the Apostles. The Waldensians, Moravians, Anabaptist, Quakers, Methodists and Pentecostals were all characterised by their missionary endeavours. There are lessons here for the churches today. We remain fundamentally weak in our emphasis on mission. Most evangelism and missions today are left to para-church groups and evangelistic organisations. Unlike the protest movements, which saw the Great Commission as the responsibility of all ordinary members, we now view this as the prerogative of specialist evangelists and missionaries. These organisations have a vital part to play in world evangelisation. But like the radical groups, we need to motivate each member of the Church to take on the responsibility of mission.

2. Pentecostal
a) The Presence of God

The power of the Holy Spirit, which was manifested in supernatural acts of God through healings and deliverance, was lost during the Catholic and Protestant eras and was replaced by earthly, civil, political and military powers. These authorities may have been fine for establishing earthly realms but they will not do for the building of God's kingdom. The presence of God dwelling in such powerful ways in the Early Church was soon lost amid the worldliness of the Catholic church. This was replaced by the splendour of ecclesiastical architecture, and mystery and wonder were introduced through the ceremonies of the altar, the liturgies, chanting and incense. The design and dimensions of the cathedrals, together with the liturgies, were created to instil a sense of awe for the worshippers. This man-made aura was a substitute for the absence of God-given awe. It would seem that when the glory of God departs, man has sought to hide his disappearance with some form of cosmetic dressing and by keeping the people in ignorance about his leave of absence. No one looking at the splendour of the Catholic Church, its wealth and power, would have dared ask: But is God still with us or is he standing outside the door of his own church as in Rev. 3:20?

The Jews during the time of Jesus were in the same situation. The grandeur of the Temple sought to hide from the ordinary people that the Ark of the Covenant was no longer in the Holy of Holies. When Jesus died on the cross and the curtain in the Temple was torn, it not only symbolised to the nation that a new way into God's presence had been made possible, it also demonstrated that God had not been dwelling in his Temple for the past 400 years. "Ichabod" (1Sam. 4:21), the glory has departed but the ordinary people were told to keep up the temple services and offerings without being informed that God's Ark was no longer there. No one stopped to ask: "Is God still with us?" - except Jesus who came as Immanuel, "God is with us", in a mobile human tabernacle dwelling in flesh and blood.

In our day, we need to pause and ask this same question: "Is God still with us or has the cloud moved on?" Are we continuing with our religious services even though the presence of God is no longer with us? Someone has made the pertinent observation that in the Early Church, 95% of their activities would have ceased if the Holy Spirit departed, whereas 95% of the activities of the

Church today would still continue even if God were to withdraw his Spirit from us. Not only are we blind if we fail to stop and ask the question. Even more of a concern is that we knowingly seek to hide his absence by stage-managing our services, adding touches of entertainment and showbiz, turning up the amplifiers in the mistaken belief that loudness equals power. Is it more important that members whose financial giving is essential for the work are sent home happy and feeling blessed than whether God is pleased with our praise and worship? Whether he is even present is in one sense an irrelevance. The Church now exists for its own entertainment, and it matters little whether we re-create the ceremonies of the medieval Church or bring in Rock music - both are substitutes; they are not edifying and will empty the churches. There is an urgent need to hand "our" churches back to God and invite his visitation. None should underestimate the threat of Jesus in Revelation 2:5: "if you do not repent, I will come to you and remove your lamp from its place." He is also in the business of closing down churches.

We have seen the way in which the Church reflects and imitates the world. The world is all geared up for entertainment, whether it be in the schools, television or music. That is what the world needs to help it to cope with life. Regrettably, our churches are becoming more and more like centres of entertainments rather than houses of prayer (Luke 19:46). Our young people do not need more entertainment. What they really need is to experience the real presence of God when the Church is gathered together. It is the reality of knowing God that will hold them to the Lord and fire them up for service. In the revival areas, young people can remember the awesomeness of God's presence when the Spirit has descended, and it has been these encounters that have kept many of them walking with God. Even those who fall away can remember those times when they touched something of his glory. And it is these memories that have brought some back. Having tasted of the new wine, they have been spoilt for anything less.

I was in a church in the West recently listening to the pastor talking excitedly about the current "move of the Spirit" and how it was affecting the life of the church. All this was very interesting but the problem was that he was preaching to a half-empty and disinterested congregation and the church had been losing numbers. Talking about revivals and "moves of the Spirit" does not mean that revival has come! The leaders of the Western churches have a great propensity to talk about these things even when there is no reality of the presence of God in their midst. This is akin to politicians talking about how the economy is improving and the country is coming out of recession when the signs of recession are evident for everyone to see.

I am often embarrassed when asked by Christians in the Far East who have experienced real revival to tell them about the revival in England. My standard response is "What revival?" The Church in the West may be better at organising conferences, may write more songs, print more books and have more money to spend on programmes for cable and satellite television, but these do not add up to revival. There have even been those who have gone to revival spots in the East to tell these Christians about the latest "move of the Spirit" in the West. The tragedy with these so called "moves of the Spirit" is that they have not resulted in evangelism and conversions. These "moves" tend to be introverted and experiential. The true presence of the Holy God is something altogether different. It leads to repentance in the Church and conversion in the world.

b) Prayer

Among charismatic churches, there is a trend towards praise-dominated services with a short time for teaching and even shorter time for prayer. Prayer is costly but praise is cosy. If we want to know the pentecostal power of the Early Church, we need to devote ourselves again to teaching and to prayer.

Churches that have experienced revival have testified to the essential place of intense prayer. The churches that are still experiencing revival are the ones where we see a seriousness about prayer. In our day, there is much talk about wanting to see

God move in revival. The question we should be asking is whether we are prepared to pay the price for revival; until we do in the area of prayer, we do not "deserve" to see revival. Many churches have prayer meetings, but few churches know how to pray and to "tarry", waiting on God. Few churches are open for God to bring conviction, and they fight shy of repentance. We preach a gospel of no condemnation for our sins (Rom. 8:1) which is right, but God still wants to bring conviction of sins; there can be no Pentecost without Calvary. When will the charismatic churches get serious about prayer? We do not need more teachings and exhortation, we have had plenty of those. What we need are men and women of prayer who can lead us into the place where we prostrate ourselves before God and cry out to him for ourselves and the state of the Church.

c) Gifts of the Spirit

There was a general cessationalist teaching that gifts ceased with the end of the apostolic age and the formation of the New Testament canon. With the cessation of the gifts, the Church also saw the end of the Body ministry in Ephesians 4. That the gifts of the Spirit did not completely die out can be seen from history as well as the present-day move of the Spirit in revival in many countries. In the 2nd century we have accounts of wandering prophets circulating the churches, exercising a charismatic ministry and complementing the ministry of resident elders. Ammia and Quadratus were two such prophets. Ignatius, Polycarp and Hermas were well aware of the continuance of prophets in their day: "The apostle believes that the prophetic charisma should continue until the end of the age throughout the Church" (Eusebius, *History* 5:17). Why then did the gifts and ministries of the Spirit apparently die out? There were four major reasons:

1) Through abuse and misuse (as in Corinth), these gifts fell into disrepute and eventually ceased to be used all together. We are seeing something of this already in some churches today. There are churches disillusioned with the exercise of spiritual gifts in ways which are banal, juvenile, repetitive and which

bear no signs of divine inspiration but all the marks of human imagination. If this misuse and abuse continues, the gifts will again fall into disrepute.

2) The Montanist movement died out at the end of the 2nd century. They began as the model and guardians of the truths concerning the spiritual gifts. However, through extremism and fanaticism and a downgrading of the Bible and exalting of prophecies, error was allowed into the Church and the work died-salutary lessons for us today.

3) There was a growing tendency to identify the prophetic function with the office of bishop. Melito and Polycarp were both bishops and prophets. After the Montanist extremism, this identification became absolute and bishops became regarded as the authoritative mouthpiece of divine teaching. "This swallowing up of the prophet in the bishop was disastrous for the Church" (Michael Green). The growth of the ecclesiastical hierarchy hindered the development of the gifts and ministries. Before long, the supernatural gifts of the Spirit were replaced by human gifts and talents; Body ministry gave way to ministry by an elite class of professional clergy.

4) Cessationalism was reinforced from the late middle ages to today by the rise of rationalism: anything which cannot be explained rationally is treated with suspicion. Thomas Aquinas combined Aristotle's ideas on using the intellect to explain the universe with the Christian idea of revelation. This laid the foundation for the scholastic movement leading eventually to an age of reasoning which questioned anything supernatural.

Among the protest movements, however, there is evidence of a more balanced attitude towards the work of the Spirit. The Waldensians emphasised the inner witness of the Spirit and maintained an apostolic ministry through the laying on of hands. The Lollards under Wycliffe saw a remarkable movement of the Holy Spirit by any account. The Huguenots in France practised "Body ministry" and spoke in tongues. The churches of Jean de Labadie in Bordeaux condemned the Synod for rejecting

1 Corinthians 14, practised community of goods and spoke in tongues. In the 1640s, the Quakers experienced and emphasised the indwelling and the anointing of the Spirit for ministry. The Moravians, who were so effective in their intercession and mission, had a clear emphasis on Body-life ministry. They experienced a "pentecost" at Herrnhut which was to spark off the greatest missionary movement of their time.

Through the 18th century, the Wesleyan revival and the Great Awakening under Jonathan Edwards saw fresh outpourings of the Spirit on the Church as thousands were converted. In the early 1900s there were two further moves of the Spirit - the Welsh revival and the Azuza Street revival. Through the Pentecostal movement, the gifts of the Spirit and Body ministry have been restored to the traditional Protestant as well as Catholic churches, and have spawned the new charismatic churches. Around the world today, there are pockets of revival in Indonesia, Borneo, Nagaland, parts of Africa, China, Korea and South America.

History therefore prompts us to ask for balance: there are churches disillusioned with the exercise of misused spiritual gifts bearing no signs of divine inspiration but all the marks of human imagination. On the other side are churches which still foster a cessationalist wing: the evangelicals among them should ask themselves whether it is not time to embrace the charismatic gifts for the extension of the Kingdom. Word and Spirit need to be joined.

d) Signs and Manifestations

There will always be a temptation for Christians to seek after signs. By nature, we are attracted to the spectacular and the unusual. But Jesus gave a warning about seeking after signs:

"An evil and adulterous generation craves for a sign; and yet no sign shall be given to it but the sign of Jonah the prophet" (Matt.12:38f).

Church history is littered with examples of extremist groups with unusual signs. There were "the shakers, the jerkers, the movers and the rollers". There were the "howlers", where the sign of the Spirit was the making of animal noises. There are still Holiness churches today where a sign of one's faith and God's anointing is the handling of poisonous snakes in the revival meetings in accordance with Mark 16: 8! What exciting meetings these must be! But are they genuine and biblical or are they manifestations of the flesh?

We have to test all such phenomena in the light of the Bible so that we may not be led astray in these days as the Scriptures has warned us (Rev.13:14; 18:23; Matt.7:15-23). In an earlier chapter on the New Testament Church, we mentioned certain features that should characterise an authentic outpouring of the Spirit. Large numbers of conversions should follow these miraculous signs. There will be conviction of sin and deep repentance. The prayer life of the Church is intensified and lives are changed. A new community results, displaying a radical love that cuts across all human barriers. This love is worked out in some form of economic sharing. To these we could add the following comments. We should become wary when certain signs become predictable. The Holy Spirit is "unpredictable", full of creativity and imagination. He does not always do things the same way. Signs should also lead to God being glorified and not men. The Spirit's role is to glorify Christ. Where men get more glory than God, we should be concerned.

Furthermore, signs are often given as a temporary phenomenon. What often begins as a genuine manifestation is taken by Christians to mean that all subsequent meetings should have the same signs. This mentality puts the Church under pressure to "reproduce" these signs or manifestations. When this happens, we move from the Spirit to the flesh, from the genuine to the imitation. The early Quakers genuinely shook when the Spirit came upon them. But this phenomenon passed, though some tried to make this a regular feature of their meetings. Today in certain charismatic churches, there is a return of the phenomenon of falling under the power of the Spirit - what has been called being "slain in the Spirit". There is no doubt that some of this is genuine. But the regularity with which one hears of people claiming they were "pushed" should cause us to remember that such manifestations may only have been intended to be once-off, and we should not try to "manufacture" them.

What is tragic is that we begin to judge meetings by the presence or absence of these manifestations. The more dramatic the manifestations, we reason, the more is the power of the Spirit. We need to be reminded that demon spirits are also capable of performing manifestations. We can see healings, speaking in tongues, prophecies, levitations and trance states in Hindu and Buddhist temples. If we crave for signs and are lacking in discernment and mature leadership in our churches, we may open ourselves to deception.

Charismatic Maturity

The Christian scene today is filled with meetings where people "come forward" for healing, blessings and "ministry". While not denying the validity of these gatherings, we need to question some of what is going on. There is a tendency among Christians for a quick-fix solution to their problems. This is the "instant Christianity" syndrome of our consumer age. Instead of repenting and turning from our sins, it is easier to go forward for prayer and the laying on of hands. We hope that God will impart his blessings and we will somehow be miraculously "zapped" to solve our problems and to live holy lives. That this does not happen - because it is contrary to Scriptures - is also evident because often the same people are the ones seeking prayer! There comes a point where prayer and the laying on of hands is no substitute for repentance and obedience. There is a confusion between the Spirit's empowering for service and for sanctification. One is instant, the other is a lifetime walk of obedience. The New Testament Christians understood this. While they were encouraged to receive the power of the Spirit for service, they were also exhorted to keep on walking faithfully with the Lord, leading holy lives. The gifts of the Spirit were balanced by teaching on the fruit of the Spirit. We need both emphases.

The renewal movement in the West has been accompanied by the mushrooming of Christian counselling for solving emotional problems. In today's psychological culture, where we need to "feel good" about ourselves, the Church is becoming more and more drawn into counselling, using all kinds of theories. Dr Larry Crabb, of the Institute of Biblical Counselling, gives a warning that should be heeded in his book *Finding God*:

> "Helping people to feel loved and worthwhile has become the central mission of the Church. We are learning not to worship God in self-denial and costly service, but to embrace our inner child, heal our memories, overcome addictions, lift our depressions, improve our self-images, establish self-preserving boundaries, substitute self-love for self-hatred, and replace shame with an affirming acceptance of who we are. Recovery from pain is absorbing an increasing share of the Church's energy. And that is alarming."

It is no longer fashionable to teach about self-control or discipline: we preach a Jesus who saves us from our hang-ups instead of our sins. It is easier to blame our problems on our past, on our society, on our parents and even on demon spirits-anything but taking the blame ourselves for wrong decisions made, wrong feelings held and lack of discipline to control our appetites. Adam blamed Eve and she blamed the serpent. Mankind has not changed much since. If it is our past, we may need counselling. If we can blame it on demon spirits, then we need deliverance. But if we have only ourselves to blame, we need repentance and obedience, which is far harder because it deals a death blow to self. We need to know the deep forgiveness of a loving and holy God who will change us gradually, from glory to glory, and help us to live more faithfully. Crabb argues that it is more important for us to find God than to try to solve our problems. I agree. When we really find God, many of our problems will disappear or become insignificant.

We need to sound the warning. Spiritual gifts do not mean spiritual maturity. The church at Corinth had more spiritual gifts than any other and yet Paul said he had to treat them as spiritual babies (1Cor. 3:1ff). Maturity requires obedience and discipline. And the radical churches would add that maturity comes through suffering as well.

3. Sacramental

a) Baptism

On the issue of baptism, the trend in church history is that from the 2nd century onwards the baptismal candidate gets younger and younger; the quantity of water gets less and less; and the height of the baptismal font gets higher and higher! From being a voluntary act of reality and power for the forgiveness of sins, baptism became a coerced ceremony with touches of magic both in the waters as well as in the rites. What is at issue here is not the form or the quantity of water. That is unimportant. I remember hearing Richard Wurmbrand, the Baptist Romanian pastor who was imprisoned for his faith for 13 years, describing how they used to baptise new converts in prison by sprinkling them with urine! Would anyone like to challenge the authenticity of their baptism? What is important is that believers should be able to renounce Satan and his works through the waters of baptism. Satan has kept Christians from the Bible for centuries because he knows how dangerous the Bible is to his activities. He has also managed to keep Christians from believers' baptism because there is power in the declaration of faith by the disciple to renounce Satan. This is why in many cultures today, new believers will start to experience persecution only when they desire to undergo believer's baptism. Every "water burial" is one more member plucked from Satan's kingdom.

Many of the radical groups understood the significance of baptism and practised believer's baptism through full immersion or sprinkling. But it is to the Anabaptists that we owe the greatest debt for preserving and restoring this truth to the Church. It is surely a sign of God's grace that there are Anglican, United Reformed and Catholic churches today practising believers' baptism. Who would have thought this was possible during the

16th century? May this trend continue so that many more will know the joy of sins forgiven and a clear conscience towards God (1Pet. 3:21)

ii) The Lord's Supper

The Lord's Supper was originally set in the context of a simple meal using everyday foods - bread and wine. It was not magical but spiritual. The bread and the wine did not magically become the literal body and blood of Christ due to the incantations of the clergy, as suggested by the doctrine of transubstantiation. The original words of Jesus to "Take, eat this is my body" were first said to the disciples when he was still alive! However, it was not merely a memorial. We do partake of the life of Christ in some mystical and spiritual way as we share in the Lord's Supper. From being a simple meal where bread and wine representing the body and blood of Jesus were eaten, the Lord's Supper took on layer upon layer of sophistication both in the ceremony and the theology during the Catholic era.

As with baptism, the trend was to turn what was simple but powerful and real into something that was sophisticated and unreal, dressing it up and in the process swapping God's power for institutional trappings. That is the danger for Catholics, whereas in other traditions the tendency is towards trivialising the things of God. Awe and reverence for God are at a low ebb in the Church today. Instead of worshipping God Almighty, we are tending to worship him as God All-matey. We are casual to the point of irreverence in our worship, prayers, handling of the Word and the sacraments: our God is a consuming fire.

Some groups (particularly the Exclusive Brethren) have restricted the table to those known to be members of the Body. Roman Catholics employ access to the sacraments as a form of discipline. Liberals are less particular allowing almost anyone to join in the Communion. And most Reformed denominations treat the Lord's Supper merely as a memorial. There remains much truth to be recovered.

4. Radical
Community

The disciples in the Early Church fulfilled the prophetic vision of the jubilee when it was said that "there were no poor among them" (Acts 4:34;cf. Deut.15:7-11). They gave themselves to acts of mercy, caring for the widows, orphans and those imprisoned. They gave sacrificially because many of the early Christians were slaves. But they determined that there should be social holiness and justice among them because they were members of the same family. This was true agapé love in action, a manifestation of heaven on earth. No wonder they described themselves as "colonies of heaven" in each city.

The practice of being family, of economic sharing was lost during the Constantinian era as the Church took on the new prosperity and wealth befitting the official religion of the Empire. From meeting in homes and catacombs, the Christians now had splendid buildings for their worship. The Church was allowed to own land and enormous estates which were either donated or bought. This change in the economic status of the church was a cause of some embarrassment. The Pope declared that Christ and the apostles were not poor and it became heretical to teach the poverty of Christ-the established churches have remained powerful economic institutions ever since.

All was not completely lost, however. The monastic movement was an attempt to return to the New Testament model of simple lifestyle and economic sharing. The likes of Francis of Assisi were wonderful characters, who sought to imitate their Lord in their simplicity and discipleship. They rediscovered brotherhood and practised economic justice among themselves. They initiated ministries to the poor and the outcast. They were to become a perennial thorn in the conscience of the established church as a reminder of its calling. Their separation from the world, however, was an over-reaction. Jesus calls us to deny the world, the flesh and the devil while still living in the world. One cannot escape the world by living in a monastery. The monastic movements' rejection of worldliness in the Church led many to adopt a life of asceticism. We may not agree entirely with the spiritual disciplines and the asceticism of the monastic movements, but have they not got something to teach us? Would not the church of today profit from a call to discipline ourselves so that we do not conform to the world? Is not discipline something that would help to curb the passion for materialism and hedonism? It is a shame that in rejecting the strict asceticism of the monastic lifestyle, we have thrown out its contributions in the areas of radical discipleship, spiritual discipline and meditation.

Economic sharing was also to be found among the radical groups. It could be argued that because the radical groups were persecuted it was easier for them to care for each other and practise economic sharing. That may be so. However, if we look at their teachings we discover that the real motivation to exercise agapé love and *koinonia* fellowship, was their understanding that they were members of a heavenly family with God as their Father. Certain groups such as the Moravians, some Anabaptists and the Hutterites went further and practised community of goods and held all things in common.

The popularity of prosperity teaching among charismatic churches is a concern. In the context of Church history, it is obvious why caution needs to be exercised with this particular form of teaching. If there were ever a time in which Christians and the Church could truly be said to be prosperous, it was during the Catholic era. But was it man's doing or God's blessing? Was it faith or was it greed? Some of the antics of the modern prosperity teachers reminds us of Tetzel, the Dominican friar whose shameless manner in the sale of indulgences finally provoked Luther's outrage. Christians are invited to send their donations in exchange for prayers and blessings. Handkerchiefs are sent so that they can be prayed over and posted back to the senders for their healing. Of course, this works better when a donation is sent in at the same time. We are told to give our offerings to these prosperity faith teachers so that we can receive it back a hundredfold. Among the latest scams is an invitation to send in a donation for every member of your family you want to become a Christian: this is indulgences charismatic-style!

Tetzel would have been quite at home in all this. Certainly the protest movements would not be able to subscribe to this kind of teaching, which can only emanate from the wealthy churches of the West. On the contrary, what we see from church history is often that the poor persecuted Christians are the ones with the real faith. Furthermore, this kind of teaching insults the vibrant churches in the poor developing nations. May it not be that prosperity teaching is a way for us to justify our lifestyle and to try to absolve a nagging conscience?

In our day we have seen many lost truths restored to the Church - salvation by faith, gifts of the Spirit, believer's baptism, authority of the Bible and so on. With the exception of certain groups, we have not seen God restoring the radical dimension to the Church at large. The world awaits a visible expression of *agapé* love, of true sharing and fellowship, of radical *koinonia* so that it may again be amazed and say: "How they love one another." Part of the meaning of the Lord's Supper is in the act of breaking the bread and in the symbolism of the wine, which both remind us of the death of Christ. But there is also meaning in the *sharing* of the loaf and cup - we are one family sharing a meal that looks forward to the Messianic Banquet to come

5. Organisational

From being a minority illegal faith in the early days, Christianity developed into the majority established faith. From being religious and political deviants, Christians became the most respectable segment of society. The real momentum for this change was the conversion of Constantine. It was unbecoming of the most powerful man on earth at that time to worship in the simplicity of the early Christians. Now that the Emperor and the upper echelons of society were going to church, it had to have the trappings of grandeur that befitted its adoption by the most powerful empire on earth. All the trappings and the buildings of the Empire were adopted by the Church after the fall of Rome. Where the devil could not destroy the Church through confrontation he did it through corruption. Satan still uses this strategy today.

In fairness, with the growth of the Church in the first three centuries there was already a trend towards some kind of institutional structure before Constantine's conversion. Charismatic lay leadership was starting to give way to clerical professional leadership in the Church. Inspirational ministry was replaced by the institutional. Above all, from a model of plurality of bishops in each church, we start to see a shift to only one bishop per church and then eventually to one bishop overseeing several churches in one region. This trend was already in place before Constantine's conversion. However, without the Emperor's endorsement, the governmental structure of the Church would not have been as sophisticated as was finally seen in Roman Catholicism. Someone has rightly observed that God always starts with a ministry which becomes a movement and then a monument. This stage was reached by the 4th century.

The independence of the first century churches became centralised until eventually all churches came under the control of one bishop, the Pope. Institutionalism is about control. Surprisingly, a similar tendency is detectable in some charismatic churches today. Though in principle they practise a plurality of leadership, closer examination reveals that there is one strong leader who tends to dominate and control the church or the movement. This desire for control saw the unhealthy growth of the "heavy shepherding movement" in the United States and Britain in the 1970s and 1980s and led to the creation of a kind of "charismatic papacy" with its own pyramid structure. This is charismatic institutionalism. Elaborate theologies were built up around Jethro's advice to Moses about appointing leaders of thousands, hundreds and tens, and the classic "Do not touch the Lord's anointed".

It is interesting how history repeats itself: the need for control is due to the insecurity of leaders and brings a gradual decline of the spontaneity and vitality of the Spirit in the Church. History teaches that this pattern of leadership is the spawning-ground of heretical cults.

To conclude the chapter, it seems that God's special interventions are a manifest part of history; but these do not occur as often as or in the way that our fallen natures would want. So that same fallenness leads us to try to make up our own "events" either in a cultic or an institutional format. But when we do this we forfeit our right to be salt and light in our generation. Can we recapture the spirit of radical Christianity as taught in the Bible and practised by the pioneers of our faith?

18

CONCLUDING REMARKS

Church history is the story of how the Church lived out its faith in the world. Some retreated into their monasteries to live out "church", while others became more and more integrated until they were part of the establishment. Still others fought bravely to be in the world but not of it. The "City of God" must coexist with the "Earthly City". Where one is emphasised to the exclusion of the other, it has proved harmful to both. These two kingdoms, while in conflict, have to continue existing in an uneasy equilibrium. Sadly, the lesson from church history is that the world has often proved stronger than the Church, and for much of the time, the Church has not been distinctly different from the world. It seems the world has usually found a way of infiltrating the Church. It is no different today. The world's materialism, injustice, indiscipline and lack of respect can be seen in the Church today.

There is much obviously that we can learn from the past. The issues and battles faced by the Church are not that different from ones we encounter today - more subtle perhaps, but essentially the same.

History is a process; it is dynamic and not static. Nothing stays the same. In the midst of enormous social and political upheavals, God's people have been able to find a Rock in their Lord and Saviour who does not change. In times of trouble, he has been their refuge and his Word has been a source of inspiration and instruction. Amid the uncertainties of our world today, the Church needs to find its way back to God and return to his Word with a fresh hunger. There will be new challenges and we can only face them when we have a sure knowledge of God and his Word.

We learn also from history that it is dangerous to presume on God's blessings. He has shown that He will move on when the Church deviates from his original intention. No segment of the Church has a monopoly on God at any time. We have also seen that God's blessings can in the end lead on to complacency and become a hindrance. His past blessings are no guarantee of his continuing presence. Every generation needs to know his presence for itself. We cannot live on the spiritual capital of the past.

Complacency is a great danger within the Church. At the peak of Israel's power during the reign of King Solomon, the nation enjoyed the bountiful blessings of God. But within a generation of his death, King Shishak from Egypt had invaded Israel and taken away all the treasures from the Temple (2 Chron. 12:9). These were the sacred things of God, made at great cost (Ex. 35-38), and part of the treasures of Israel. King Rehoboam then substituted the golden shields taken by King Shishak with some bronze replicas. We have here a lesson confirmed by Church history. When the early Church became complacent and thought that it had arrived, the enemy entered and took away its treasures-as we have seen, the Church was robbed of many truths for a very long time. Instead of recovering the "golden" truths however, it often settled for poor quality "bronze" replicas of the real thing. In our day, complacency is still a major threat and unless we are watchful and seek to walk humbly with our God, we too face the same danger.

We also need to look to God to restore other truths to the Church. The issue of radical discipleship and lifestyle has been mentioned. From the Catholic tradition, there is the challenge of the monastic movements. Furthermore, I believe that in our day, we need to recover a love for the mystics. These were Christians who touched depths of devotion to God and whose experience of the Holy One is foreign to the modern Church. We need them to lead us into a much deeper devotion of our God that will enrich our individual and corporate worship. It is indeed sad that the modern Christian knows little of the writings and hymns of mystics, both ancient, such as Bernard of Clairvaux, Tauler and Fenelon, as well as "recent", such as Faber, Watts and Tozer. This is our loss and the Church is the poorer without their contribution.

This brief survey should make us grow in our appreciation of the richness of God's work across history. We will be less inclined in the future to imagine that everything exciting began with us! We should see now that we have many spiritual ancestors. This should both humble and excite us. We are the product of many streams, and more and more we are seeing these converging. Catholicism today acknowledges the necessity of faith and honours preaching, but the centre of its religious life is in the sacraments rather than the sermon. Classical Protestantism, especially in its Lutheran form, ascribes value to the sacraments, but its emphasis is on an evangelical faith through the preaching. Pentecostalism values both the sacraments and the sermon but sees the work of the Holy Spirit as of paramount importance in every aspect of Church life. We are inheritors of these truths. To that we need the merging of the Radicals' stream with their emphasis on discipleship, community and non-institutional forms of church government. As we have seen, distortions have resulted from taking any one of these emphases alone as characteristic of the nature of the Church. It is only when all these features are present, that we will see the kind of Church which Jesus intended.

How do we keep movements fresh, alive and on the rails? How do we prevent dynamic groups from settling down and becoming independent of God? Perhaps it is impossible; it is human nature to settle down and enjoy what has been gained. Looking at Church history, I am pessimistic as to whether any movement can stay fresh and dynamic over several generations. Perhaps it is God's intention that in every generation, there should be a fresh movement of the Spirit.

It is difficult to summarise such a wide sweep of history, but if there is one overriding lesson we need to learn, it is this: we are a pilgrim church called to a walk of faith. While on this journey, we should learn to be less dogmatic, more loving; less bigoted, more humble. Above all, we should have a real hunger for the Lord Jesus; seek to love Him with all our hearts and minds and to love our neighbour as ourselves. We should get on with the task of mission and get the Bride ready. He is coming back. Maranatha! Come, Lord Jesus, come!

APPENDICES

GLOSSARY

Apologist   Defenders of the Christian faith who wrote against paganism and Judaism.

Catechumen   Someone undergoing instruction to prepare for water baptism.

Creed   A statement summarising aspects of the faith. There have been various creeds formulated, often to combat error. The Apostles' Creed and Nicene Creed are examples.

Didache   Literally means "teaching" and is a document containing instructions on church organisation, worship and moral behaviour. Probably from the early 2nd century, of Syriac origins.

Eastern Church   The Church in the eastern part of the Mediterranean and beyond. Largely influenced by Greek culture.

Eucharist   The name used by the Early Church fathers for the communion service. It comes from the Greek word for thanksgiving.

Indulgences   The granting of pardon for sins drawing upon the merit of the good deeds of the saints. Since the sinner is unable to carry out sufficient penance for the remission of his sins, he is able to draw on the "spiritual treasury" of good deeds formed by Christ, the Virgin Mary and the saints. Most indulgences were granted by the Pope and were applicable to the souls in purgatory. The sale of indulgences became the means of raising money for the papacy's activities.

Mariolatry	The worship of Mary as the Mother of God.
Metropolitan	Bishop of a major city accorded a higher status and rank than other bishops. Each became the sole bishop of each city presiding over several congregations.
Patriarch	The title given to the bishops of the five dominant churches during the Early Church– Rome, Constantinople, Antioch, Jerusalem and Alexandria.
Presbyter	Greek word for elder.
Purgatory	A place of temporal punishment where departed souls have to endure punishment for their sins. This is not hell, because all the souls in purgatory are on their way to heaven. Release from purgatory can come through their purgatory suffering, or can be obtained by the purchase of indulgences or acts of penance.
Simony	The conferral and acquisition of spiritual blessings and benefits by monetary means like that attempted by Simon Magus (Acts 8:18-24). Its classic expression was the medieval sale of clerical offices.
Vulgate	The revision of the Latin version of the Bible by Jerome (c.347-420). It gradually became the standard version of the Bible in Latin.
Western Church	The church in the western part of the Mediterranean. Largely influenced by Roman (or Latin) culture.

EARLY CHURCH LEADERS

Clement of Rome (fl.ca.90-100)

The prominent presbyter-bishop of Rome probably mentioned in Phil. 4:3. He is most probably the Clement in Hermas's Shepherd whose duty was to write to the other churches. He is credited with the authorship of 1 Clement, a letter from the church in Rome to the church in Corinth. He was executed by Emperor Domitian.

Justin Martyr (ca.100-165)

Born in Shechem, Palestine, he was a student of philosophy and became a Christian through a conversation with an old man in Ephesus. He came to Rome and continued with his preaching. He wrote two Apologies, explaining the Christian faith to unbelievers. He was arrested and executed with six friends during a wave of anti-Christian feeling in Rome.

Tatian (ca.110-172)

Born in Syria, he came to Rome in 150 where he was converted and later became a pupil of Justin Martyr. He returned to Syria and was an effective apologist engaged in the defence of the faith against Greek philosophies. His main work was the Diatessaron, a single account of Christ compiled from the four gospels. He made a significant contribution to the Syriac-speaking churches.

Irenaeus (ca.130-c.200)

From Smyrna (Turkey), a pupil of Polycarp. After the persecution of 177, he became Bishop of Lyons in France. He wrote five books called Against Heresy to deal with the various forms of Gnosticism.

Tertullian (ca.160-ca.215)

Known almost exclusively through his writings, of which 31 Latin works survived but none of his Greek ones. Based in Carthage, he was a prolific and brilliant writer covering doctrines and church practices, but was at his best in apologetics. In 207, he broke with the mainstream church and joined the Montanists. He is regarded as one of the intellectual giants of history and called the "father of

Latin theology".

Origen (ca.185-253)

Was born of Christian parents in Alexandria. He was perhaps the greatest Christian scholar and preacher of the Early Church. From youth, he had a genuine zeal for the gospel. When his father was arrested, he wanted to accompany him to prison so as to encourage him. Origen was only stopped because his mother hid his clothes, such was his devotion. His contribution to biblical scholarship is immense. He wrote more than 6,000 pamphlets, tracts and books. He compiled parallel versions of the Hebrew and Greek Old Testament, a large work on systematic theology and a vast number of sermons and commentaries. He was imprisoned and tortured during the persecution of Emperor Decius and died a few years later as a result of his sufferings.

Athanasius (ca.295-373)

Theologian and bishop of Alexandria. He was the leading opponent of Arius' teachings and was instrumental in the outcome of the Council of Nicea, called to resolve this doctrinal controversy.

SUMMARY TABLE POST-REFORMATION RADICALS

DATE	RADICAL	MAINLINE	Everymember evangelism	Ecstatic utterance	Believers' baptism	Political radicalism
AD 1500	Anabaptists (p167,178)	Early Luther	✓	✓	✓	✓
	Mennonites (page 179)		✓	✓		✓
AD 1600	Quakers (page 189)			✓	✓	✓
	Baptists (page 188)			✓	✓	
AD 1700	Moravians (page 190)	Methodists (page 192)	✓		✓	✓
AD 1800	Apostolic	Brethren / Salvation Army		✓	✓	
AD 1900	Pentecostal			✓	✓	✓
		Charismatic			✓	✓

Note: Ticks refer to the 'radical' column; the 'mainline' column refers to anti-institutional sentiment which did not go as far as abandoning infant baptism or risking being branded as heretical or unpatriotic.

SUMMARY TABLE
PRE-REFORMATION
RADICALS

DATE	RADICAL	MAINLINE	Everymember evangelism	Ecstatic utterance	Believers' baptism	Political radicalism
AD 200	Montanists (page 90)		✓	✓	✓	✓
AD 300	Novatians (page 93)		✓			
AD 400	Donatists (page 94) Priscillians (page 95)	Desert Fathers	✓ ✓	?		
AD 500	Paulicians (page 110)		✓	✓		
600 - 800						
AD 900	Bogomiles (page 112)					✓
AD 1000	Albigenses (page 127)		✓	✓		✓
AD 1100	Waldensian (page 131)		✓		✓	✓
AD 1200		Franciscans (page 129)				
AD 1300	Lollards Hussites (page 133) (page 136)	Thomas à Kempis (page 141)	✓		✓	
AD 1400	Unitas Fratrum Hutterites (Page 138)		✓			✓

EARLY PRECURSORS OF RADICAL MOVEMENTS (UNTIL 1000)

Britain
& Rome:
Pelagius
(p. 104)

Rome:
Novatian
(p. 93)

Armenia,
Balkans:
Paulicians (p.110)

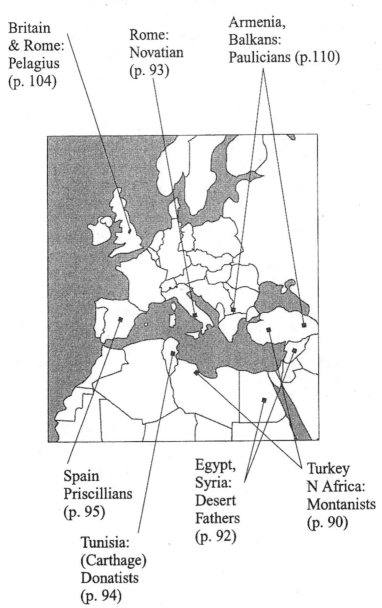

Spain
Priscillians
(p. 95)

Egypt,
Syria:
Desert
Fathers
(p. 92)

Turkey
N Africa:
Montanists
(p. 90)

Tunisia:
(Carthage)
Donatists
(p. 94)

RADICAL POST-REFORMATION MOVEMENTS (UNTIL 1800)

England:

Quakers
(p.189) &
Methodists
(p.192)

Netherlands,
N. Germany:
Menno
Simmons
Mennonites
(p.179)

Austria,
(Czech)
Moravia:
Zinzendorf
(p.190)

migrants

Baptists
in Rhode Island
Roger Williams
(p.206)

Anabaptists
of Bohemia:
Hutterites (p.176)

Anabaptists
at Munster
in Westphalia:
John of Leyden
(p.178)

Anabaptists of Zurich,
Switzerland:
Manz & Blaurock
(p.167)

PRE-REFORMATION PROTEST GROUPS

England:
Wycliffe
& the
Lollards
(p. 133)

Netherlands:
Thomas à
Kempis &
Brethren of
the Common
Life   (p. 140)

(Czech)
Bohemia:
Jan Hus
Unitas
Fratrum
(p.136)

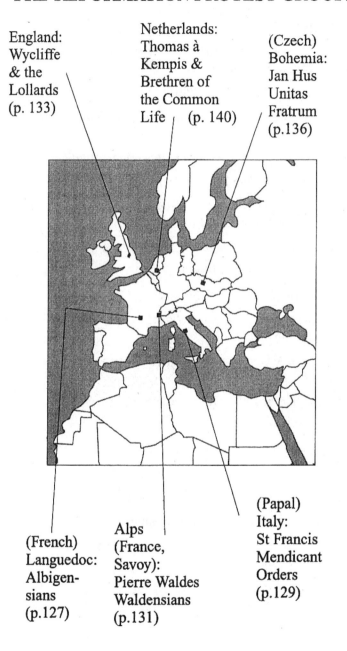

(French)
Languedoc:
Albigen-
sians
(p.127)

Alps
(France,
Savoy):
Pierre Waldes
Waldensians
(p.131)

(Papal)
Italy:
St Francis
Mendicant
Orders
(p.129)

BIBLIOGRAPHY

Atkinson J. *Martin Luther and the Birth of Protestantism,* Marshall Morgan & Scott

Bainton R. *Here I Stand,* Lion Publishing

Bettenson H (Ed). *Documents of the Christian Church,* Oxford University Press

Broadbent EH. *The Pilgrim Church,* Pickering & Inglis

Bruce FF. *The Spreading Flame,* Paternoster Press

Burgess SM & McGee GB (Eds). *Dictionary of Pentecostal and Charismatic Movement,* Grand Rapids/Zondervan

Chadwick H. *The Early Church,* Penguin Books

Cullmann O. *Early Church Worship,* SCM

Cullmann O. *State in the New Testament,* SCM

Douglas JD(Ed). *The New International Dictionary of the Christian Church,* Paternoster Press

Dowley T(Ed). A *Lion Handbook on the History of Christianity,* Lion Publishing

Durnbaugh DF. *The Believers'* Church, Macmillan

Estep W. *The Anabaptist Story,* Eerdmans

Estep W. *Renaissance & Reformation,* Eerdmans

Ferguson E. *Early Christians Speak,* Biblical Research Press

Goertz, *Profiles of Radical Reformers,* Herald Press

Hutton JE. *A History of the Moravian Church,* Moravian Publication

Koenigsberger HG & Mosse GL. E*urope in the Sixteenth Century,* Longmans

Latourette KS. *History of Expansion of Christianity*, Paternoster Press

Latourette KS. *Christianity in a Revolutionary Age,* Paternoster Press

Lightfoot JB. *The Apostolic Fathers,* Baker

Lind M. *Yahweh is a Warrior,* Herald Press

Neill S. A *History of Christian Missions,* Penguin Books

Newbigin L. *The Household of Faith,* SCM Press

Paternoster Church History, Paternoster Press

Skevington-Wood A. *The Burning Heart,* Paternoster Press

Smith MA. From *Christ to Constantine,* Inter-Varsity Press

Stevenson J. A *New Eusebius,* SPCK

Verduin L. *The Reformers and Their Stepchildren*, Baker

Verduin L. *The Anatomy of a Hybrid,* Baker

Williams GH. *The Radical Reformation,* Westminster Press